80+ NICE
RICE
RECIPES
FROM ASIA

Smith
Street
Books

10
STEAMED

48
FRIED

74
SIMMERED

96
MOULDED

122
SWEET

140
BASICS

INTRODUCTION

We aren't sure exactly when rice cultivation started, or exactly where, but the grain has shaped human history and many delicious meals. For thousands of years, we've relied on rice as a staple food source, entire cuisines revolving around it.

Today, rice is cultivated globally, but no other continent produces or consumes as much as Asia, where rice is the foundation of early breakfasts, quick lunches, mid-afternoon snacks and evening feasts.

This book contains a small sample of the wide world of rice, with dishes written by a collection of chefs. The origins of the recipes are scattered throughout Asia, and include the Philippines, China, Japan, Korea, Vietnam, Thailand, Malaysia, Singapore, Laos, Sri Lanka and India. Food borders are amorphous, and some of these dishes are shared by multiple countries with a common culinary heritage; others have a hometown and specific story that brought them to our tables. All of them are delicious.

The Simmered chapter includes dishes to start the day and end the night with, from Arroz caldo (page 83) to Khao tom (page 78). When you want to impress guests, flip to the Steamed chapter to prepare Chirashi (page 12) or enjoy a quick meal alone with a bowl of Oyakodon (page 29). If you're packing lunch for a day out, try the Moulded chapter for recipes like Onigiri (page 110) and Chi fan (page 115), or celebrate a special occasion (or just a weeknight evening) with Pearl meatballs (page 104). Flip to the Fried chapter if you have left-over rice, and prepare it with garlic to make Tapsilog (page 54), or toss in some char siu to make Yeung chau chow fan (page 60). And if you're craving something between meals, check the Sweet chapter to whip up some chocolate Champorado (page 129) or chop some pistachios for Kheer (page 132).

Rice invites you steam and fry your way through these recipes and many more. Stock up on different varieties of rice and revisit favourite dishes, discover new staples and enjoy a umami-filled exploration of your local Asian supermarket.

GLOSSARY

When in doubt, just head to your local Asian supermarket for these ingredients.

BELACAN
This staple of Peranakan and Malay cuisine is made from krill (tiny shrimp-like crustaceans) that have been salted, dried and fermented, which yields a deep salty-umami. Toast raw belacan in a dry frying pan before using for best results.

DRIED SHRIMP
Common across Asian cuisines, sun-dried shrimp are popular for their unique taste that packs a sweet umami. Shrunk to the size of a thumbnail, their flavour is a whole lot larger.

GHEE
Common to Indian kitchens, ghee is created by clarifying butter, giving it a nuttier flavour and a higher smoking point.

GOCHUGARU
These Korean chilli flakes (also called Korean chilli powder), are widely used in Korean dishes. Gochugaru usually comes in two forms: coarse chilli flakes or fine powder.

GOCHUJANG
Gochujang is a spicy-sweet fermented chilli paste widely used in Korean cuisine. Try it once and you'll keep it stocked in your fridge forever.

HONDASHI
While dashi – the stock essential to Japanese cooking – is easy to make at home, Hondashi makes the process even easier. The powder is simply mixed with water to create a simple broth: perfect for when you're in a rush.

LAP CHEONG
Known as Chinese sausage, lap cheong covers a wide range of preserved sausages, most often made with pork. While they can be eaten without preparation, a few slices added to a dish will add a salty-sweet flavour.

MIRIN
A rice wine common in Japanese cooking, with an alcohol content lower than sake's. Mirin brings a sweeter note to dishes, with a subtle hit of tang.

PALM SUGAR
A sugar derived from coconut palm sap. It's less sweet than white or brown sugar and adds a rich, smoky note that's similar to caramel.

PANDAN LEAVES
Popular across Southeast Asia, this aromatic ingredient is added to both sweet and savoury dishes. Commonly compared to vanilla, though with grassier notes, pandan leaves are sold fresh, frozen and dried.

SESAME PASTE
Though it's also made from sesame seeds, this paste is much thicker than tahini. The seeds are toasted, which create the paste's nutty, aromatic quality.

SHAOXING RICE WINE
This rice wine is key to Chinese cooking, used in dishes ranging from soups to wontons. It adds a complexity to dishes, introducing a rich, nutty flavour that creates a depth in anything you add it to.

SHICHIMI TOGARASHI
A Japanese spice mixture containing seven ingredients – red chilli pepper, sansho pepper, hemp seeds and/or poppy seeds, sesame seeds, ginger, citrus peel and nori. It's a welcome seasoning on rice dishes (or anything else you're inspired to sprinkle it on).

TAMARIND
Used dried, as a sauce, and in pastes: the pulp from the tamarind fruit has many purposes. It's popular across Asian cuisines for the sour and sweet to tangy and tart flavours it can add to a dish.

CHIRASHIZUSHI

Although some bowls of Chirashi boast brilliant displays of sashimi, raw fish is not essential to this Japanese dish. Always present, though, is a rainbow of colourful ingredients, arranged on a bed of vinegared rice. Here, cooked prawns (shrimp) sit among bright pops of edamame, tuna and ikura (salmon roe), everything resting upon strips of omelette to create a variety of tastes and textures.

RECIPE BY BILLY LAW

SERVES 4

3 large eggs

1 tsp salt

1 tbsp neutral oil

100 g (3½ oz) edamame

180 g (6½ oz) prawns (shrimp), peeled and deveined

555 g (3 cups) prepared sushi rice (page 103)

2 tsp toasted white sesame seeds, plus extra to serve

150 g (5½ oz) sashimi-grade tuna, cut into 2 cm (¾ in) cubes

100 g (3½ oz) ikura (salmon roe)

1 avocado, cut into 1 cm (½ in) cubes

soy sauce, for dipping

wasabi, to serve

Whisk the eggs and salt in a bowl until fluffy. Heat the oil in a large non-stick frying pan over medium–low heat. Pour in the egg mixture and swirl the pan to spread evenly, then cook the egg until the top is slightly dry and the edges are lifted from the pan. Jiggle the pan slightly to dislodge the omelette and flip over to cook for another 15 seconds. Transfer the omelette to a cutting board to cool, then roll into a log and slice into thin strips. Set aside.

Meanwhile, bring a saucepan of water to the boil and fill two bowls with iced water. Blanch the edamame in the boiling water for 1 minute, then transfer to a bowl of iced water. Drop the prawns in the boiling water and cook for 1 minute, then transfer to the second bowl of iced water. Drain both and set aside.

Place the sushi rice in a large serving bowl and use the back of a rice paddle to level the top. Sprinkle the sesame seeds over the rice, then fully cover it with a bed of the egg. Arrange the prawns, tuna, ikura, edamame and avocado on top. Sprinkle with more sesame seeds and serve with soy sauce and wasabi on the side.

NASI LEMAK

Fragrant coconut rice cooked with pandan leaves is the foundation of this Malaysian breakfast staple and national icon. Piled on and around it is a crunchy, umami hit of sambal, eggs, cucumbers, fried peanuts and dried anchovies. Different accompaniments are common, but this recipe features the traditional spread.

RECIPE BY AIM ARIS & AHMAD SALIM

SERVES 4

400 g (2 cups) basmati or long-grain rice

250 ml (1 cup) coconut cream

5 cm (2 in) piece ginger, sliced

1 tsp salt

2 pandan leaves, knotted

SAMBAL

2 large red onions, sliced

3 garlic cloves, sliced

15 dried chillies, soaked in water for 15 minutes

30 g (1 cup) dried anchovies

2.5 cm (1 in) piece toasted belacan (shrimp paste)

200 ml (7 fl oz) neutral oil

2 tbsp sugar, plus extra if needed

1 tbsp tamarind paste

TO SERVE

hard-boiled eggs, halved, or fried eggs, sunny side up

sliced cucumbers

fried peanuts

fried dried anchovies

To make the sambal, place the red onion, garlic, dried chillies, dried anchovies, belacan and half of the oil in a food processor or blender and process to form a paste.

Pour the remaining oil into a frying pan and heat over medium heat. Add the chilli paste and cook for 4–5 minutes, stirring regularly, until it turns a darker shade of red and the oil has separated.

Add the sugar and cook for another minute to let it caramelise with the sambal. Add the tamarind paste and 125 ml (½ cup) of water and cook, stirring, for 3 minutes or until the sambal has thickened slightly. Season to taste with salt and extra sugar if needed. Keep in mind that the sambal should be a good balance of sweet, spicy and sour flavours.

Wash the rice until the water runs clear, then transfer to a rice cooker. Add the coconut cream and 500 ml (2 cups) of water and stir in the ginger, salt and pandan leaves. Leave to soak for 5–10 minutes, then switch the rice cooker on and cook the rice according to the manufacturer's instructions.

Lightly fluff up the cooked rice. Serve immediately with the sambal, egg, cucumber, peanuts and dried anchovies.

NOTE: Any left-over sambal will keep in an airtight container in the fridge for up to 5 days.

A well-loved vegetable in Japan, the eggplant (aubergine) is the star of this vegan dish. A bed of rice is topped with rich, tender slices of soy sauce- and mirin-glazed eggplant, which is then sprinkled with sesame seeds and spring onion (scallion).

RECIPE BY BILLY LAW

SERVES 2

1 (200g) Japanese or Lebanese eggplant (aubergine), cut lengthways into 3–4 mm (⅛ in) slices

75 g (½ cup) plain (all-purpose) flour

2 tbsp neutral oil, plus extra if needed

steamed short-grain rice, to serve

1 spring onion (scallion), finely sliced

toasted white sesame seeds, to garnish

SEASONING

1 tbsp miso paste

2 tbsp hon mirin (cooking sake)

1 tbsp granulated sugar

1 tbsp soy sauce

1 tbsp grated ginger

Place the eggplant slices on a large tray and sprinkle salt on both sides, then leave to dehydrate for 20 minutes.

Meanwhile, mix all the seasoning ingredients with 125 ml (½ cup) of water in a bowl until the sugar dissolves. Set aside.

Use paper towel to dry the eggplant and wipe off any excess moisture. Spread the flour out in a small tray, and one at a time, dust the eggplant slices in flour until evenly coated.

Heat the oil in a large non-stick frying pan over medium heat. Add the eggplant slices in a single layer and fry for 3–4 minutes, until golden. Flip the slices over and fry the other side for 3 minutes; add more oil if the eggplant sticks to the bottom of the pan.

Drizzle over the seasoning and bring to a simmer. Reduce the heat to low and braise the eggplant until the sauce has reduced by half and thickened. Baste the eggplant with the sauce occasionally so it is nicely coated.

Divide the rice between serving bowls. Place the braised eggplant on top of the rice and drizzle with some of the sauce. Garnish with the spring onion and sesame seeds.

EGGPLANT DONBURI

BIBIMBAP

Korean for 'mixed rice', Bibimbap is just that – a bowl of rice served with toppings, everything mixed at the table. There's no strict rule for which toppings to add, but each should be prepared separately, bringing out the best of the ingredients. This recipe keeps things simple, but you can add more toppings if you like.

RECIPE BY BILLY LAW

SERVES 4

2 tbsp neutral oil

4 eggs

steamed short-grain rice, to serve

Sauteed zucchini (page 146), to serve

Seasoned English spinach (page 146), to serve

Seasoned soybean sprouts (page 147), to serve

Bibim sauce (page 142), to serve

BEEF BULGOGI

220 g (8 oz) beef rib eye or scotch fillet

1 tbsp soy sauce

2 tsp caster (superfine) sugar

2 tsp sesame oil

3 garlic cloves, finely chopped

1 tsp toasted sesame seeds

To make the beef bulgogi, slice the beef into 5 mm (¼ in) thick strips and add them to a bowl with the soy sauce, sugar, sesame oil, garlic and sesame seeds. Mix until well combined, then set aside to marinate for 20 minutes.

Heat the oil in a non-stick frying pan over medium–high heat. Fry the eggs, sunny side up, for about 2 minutes, then remove and set aside. In the same pan, stir-fry the beef for 4–5 minutes, until browned. Remove from the heat and leave to cool to room temperature.

To assemble the bibimbap, divide the rice between serving bowls. Arrange the vegetables and beef over the rice, then place a fried egg on top. Serve with a big dollop of the bibim sauce on the side.

The simplicity of Shanghai vegetable rice makes it a perfect choice for easy home cooking, especially when you're after something comforting. Despite a name that implies a vegetarian option, this dish features lap cheong (Chinese sausage), which pairs with the bok choy (pak choy) and rice for a complete meal in one bowl.

RECIPE BY BILLY LAW

SERVES 4

6 dried shiitake mushrooms

400 g (2 cups) short- or medium-grain rice

1 tbsp neutral oil

3 lap cheong (Chinese sausages), diced into 1 cm (½ in) cubes

5 garlic cloves, finely chopped

8 baby bok choy (pak choy), about 300 g (10½ oz), stalks removed, leaves finely cut, white and green parts separated

1½ tsp salt

1 tsp granulated sugar

½ tsp ground white pepper

2 tsp sesame oil

Soak the mushrooms in boiling water for 30 minutes. Squeeze to remove excess water and dice into small pieces. Set aside.

Meanwhile, wash the rice until the water runs clear, then cook in a rice cooker according to the manufacturer's instructions.

Heat the oil in a wok over medium–high heat. Add the lap cheong and stir-fry for 1 minute. Add the mushroom and stir-fry for another minute. Reduce the heat to medium, add the garlic and saute for about 30 seconds, until fragrant. Add the bok choy, white part only, and stir-fry for about 1 minute, until softened, then add the green part and stir-fry for 30 seconds. Add the remaining ingredients and stir fry for 15 seconds to mix well.

Add the stir-fry to the rice cooker. Using a rice paddle, mix everything together until well combined. Close the lid and leave on the 'keep warm' setting for another 5 minutes, then serve.

Although Hainanese chicken rice is originally from Hainan in southern China, the dish travelled with migrants to other countries, including Thailand, where it evolved into Khao mun gai. The dish didn't migrate far in terms of preparation, though, as it still features poached chicken and – the highlight of the dish – rice cooked in flavoursome chicken fat and an aromatic stock.

RECIPE BY SAREEN ROJANAMETIN & JEAN THAMTHANAKORN

SERVES 6

1 whole ginger root, sliced diagonally

1 Chinese cabbage (wombok), roughly chopped

5 coriander (cilantro) roots, scraped clean

20 white peppercorns

2 tbsp soy sauce

2 pandan leaves, knotted

1 × 2.5–3 kg (5 lb 8 oz– 6 lb 10 oz) free-range chicken

3 tbsp fine sea salt

3 tbsp caster (superfine) sugar

Soy dipping sauce (page 143), to serve

RICE

500 g (1 lb 2 oz) chicken skin, roughly chopped

1 Asian shallot, finely sliced

30 g (1 oz) garlic cloves, roughly chopped

5 cm (2 in) piece ginger, sliced diagonally

400 g (2 cups) jasmine rice

1 tsp fine sea salt

1 tsp caster sugar

1 pandan leaf, knotted

Bring 6 litres (6 qts) of water to the boil in a large stockpot over high heat and add the ginger, cabbage, coriander roots, peppercorns, soy sauce and pandan leaves. Carefully add the chicken and reduce the heat to medium–low. Add the salt and sugar and simmer for approximately 45 minutes, until the chicken is cooked through.

Fill a large bowl with iced water and remove the stockpot from the heat. Using tongs, transfer the chicken to the iced water. Once cool, drain and remove any excess moisture with paper towel. Scoop out any fat on the surface of the stock. Rub the chicken skin with a little of the fat to prevent it from drying out and reserve the stock and remaining fat.

To make the rice, render the chicken skin in a wok over medium heat for 30–40 minutes, stirring occasionally and reducing the heat if it darkens too quickly, until it is golden brown and the fat has rendered out. Transfer the skin with a slotted spoon to drain on paper towel (use it to garnish other dishes). Saute the shallot in the oil for 4–5 minutes. Strain through a fine-mesh sieve into a bowl. Discard the shallot.

In a clean wok, heat 80 ml (⅓ cup) of the chicken skin oil over medium heat and stir-fry the garlic and ginger until fragrant. Add the rice and stir to coat with the oil, then pour in 30 g (1 oz) of the chicken fat from the stock, along with the salt and sugar. Add 250 ml (1 cup) of the stock and stir-fry until the rice turns a cloudy white. Remove from the heat.

Place the pandan leaf in a rice cooker and cover with the rice. Add enough stock to cover the rice by about 2 cm (¾ in) and cook according to the manufacturer's instructions. Once done, leave on the 'keep warm' setting, lid on, for 15–20 minutes, then remove the ginger and pandan leaf. Stir to thoroughly mix and transfer to a serving plate.

Dilute the remaining stock with water to taste, bring to the boil and ladle into small serving bowls. Carve the chicken into 1 cm (½ in) slices and arrange on top of the rice. Serve with dipping sauce and the bowls of stock.

LU ROU FAN

In Taiwan, Lu rou fan (and its close relative rou zao fan) are easy to find. This popular street food isn't expensive, but the experience of eating it is truly luxurious – richly spiced pork belly braised until tender and served with eggs cooked in the same broth. A savoury and sweet sauce coats the pork, which sits on a bed of rice, with blanched vegetables offering a complementary crunch.

RECIPE BY BILLY LAW

SERVES 4–6

2–3 hard-boiled eggs, peeled

steamed jasmine rice, to serve

blanched baby bok choy (pak choy), to serve (optional)

BRAISED PORK BELLY

250 ml (1 cup) neutral oil

130 g (4½ oz) Asian shallots, finely sliced

500 g (1 lb 2 oz) pork belly, skin on, cut into thin strips

5 garlic cloves, finely sliced

2 tbsp granulated sugar

2 tbsp soy sauce

1 tbsp dark soy sauce

2 tbsp Shaoxing rice wine

½ tsp Chinese five-spice

1 tsp ground white pepper

To make the braised pork belly, heat the oil in a wok over medium–high heat. Fry the shallot for about 3 minutes, until golden and crispy. Drain the oil through a fine-mesh sieve and set the fried shallot aside. Any left-over oil will keep in an airtight container in the fridge for up to 5 days.

Fry the pork in a Dutch oven over medium–high heat for about 5 minutes until the juice has evaporated, the fat starts to render and the meat is slightly browned. Add the garlic and fry for a minute until fragrant. Add the fried shallots, remaining pork belly ingredients and 500 ml (2 cups) of water, stir well and bring to a simmer. Reduce the heat to low, add the eggs and cover, leaving the pork to braise for an hour. Remove the lid and braise uncovered for another 10 minutes to reduce the sauce slightly.

Remove the eggs with a slotted spoon and halve them.

Serve the braised pork over rice with baby bok choy, if desired, and an egg half.

D A L
B H A T

Lentils and rice are at the heart of this Nepalese staple. Often fed to hikers trekking the Himalayas, Dal bhat is a hearty dish flavoured with a warming mix of spices. This recipe is served with tarkari and greens, but other popular sides include chutney and pickles.

RECIPE BY CAROLINE GRIFFITHS

SERVES 4

200 g (1 cup) masoor dal (split red lentils), rinsed

2 tbsp ghee

1 onion, chopped

½ tsp ground coriander

½ tsp ground cumin

½ tsp chilli powder

½ tsp ground turmeric

¼ tsp ground cardamom

¼ tsp ground cinnamon

pinch of ground cloves

stir-fried mustard greens, to serve

steamed basmati rice, to serve

VEGETABLE TARKARI

2 tbsp ghee

2 onions, chopped

1–2 long green chillies, split lengthways, to taste

1 fresh or dried bay leaf

3 garlic cloves, crushed

2.5 cm (1 in) piece ginger, finely grated

2 tsp cumin seeds

1 tsp coriander seeds

¼ tsp ground turmeric

2 potatoes, peeled, cut into 1.5 cm (½ in) pieces

½ cauliflower, cut into small florets

3 tomatoes, quartered

120 g (1 cup) edamame

coriander (cilantro) leaves, to serve (optional)

Combine the masoor dal with ½ tsp of salt and 375 ml (1½ cups) of water in a saucepan over medium heat and bring to the boil. Reduce the heat to a low simmer, then cover, leaving the lid open a crack, and cook, stirring occasionally, for 20–25 minutes, until the lentils are soft and broken down. Add a little boiling water if the mixture starts to stick to the bottom of the pan or is becoming too thick.

Meanwhile, prepare the vegetable tarkari. Heat the ghee in a large saucepan over medium–low heat. Add the onion and cook, stirring occasionally, for 8–10 minutes, until golden. Add the chillies, bay leaf, garlic, ginger and spices, along with a good pinch of salt, and cook for 1–2 minutes, until fragrant. Add the potato and cook, stirring occasionally, for 4–5 minutes, until the potato starts to brown. Add the cauliflower, tomato and 250 ml (1 cup) of water. Bring to the boil, then reduce the heat and simmer for 10 minutes. Add the edamame and cook for a further 5 minutes, or until the vegetables are tender. Taste and season generously with black pepper and a little more salt if necessary.

While the tarkari simmers, heat the ghee in a small frying pan over medium heat. Add the onion and cook, stirring occasionally, for 8–10 minutes, until golden. Add the spices and cook for 2–3 minutes, until fragrant. Stir the spice mixture into the finished dal.

Scatter the tarkari with coriander leaves, if desired. In separate dishes, serve the dal, vegetable tarkari, mustard greens and rice.

While Oyakodon is widely available in restaurants and convenience stores in Japan, this easy-to-make donburi is commonly made at home. The bites of chicken and softly set egg are cooked with onions in a broth, then served on a bed of rice. Umami-rich, this is Japanese comfort food at its best.

RECIPE BY BILLY LAW

SERVES 2

2 boneless chicken thighs, skin on, cut into bite-size pieces

1 tbsp hon mirin (cooking sake)

½ onion, sliced lengthways

3 large eggs, at room temperature

5 sprigs mitsuba (see Note), roughly chopped

steamed short-grain rice, to serve

shichimi togarashi, to serve (optional)

SAUCE

10 g (¼ oz) Hondashi (dashi powder), mixed with 250 ml (1 cup) water

2 tbsp soy sauce

2 tbsp mirin

1 tsp caster (superfine) sugar

Add the chicken and hon mirin to a bowl, stir and set aside to marinate for 5 minutes.

To make the sauce, add all the ingredients to a bowl and stir until the sugar dissolves, then set aside.

Heat a small non-stick frying pan over medium–high heat. Place the marinated chicken skin-side down in a single layer and brown the skin for 3–4 minutes, until golden and crispy. Remove from the pan and set aside.

Reduce the heat to medium and, to the same pan, add the onion and sauce. Bring to a simmer, then distribute the chicken evenly over the onion. Continue to simmer for 3–5 minutes, turning the chicken at the halfway mark, until cooked through.

Meanwhile, crack the eggs into a bowl. Using chopsticks or a fork, beat the eggs a few times – just enough to break the yolks without fully incorporating the whites. Pour two-thirds of the egg around the pan with the chicken and leave undisturbed for 30 seconds. Add the remaining egg and sprinkle over half of the mitsuba, then reduce the heat to the lowest setting and cook for another 30 seconds. Turn the heat off, cover the pan, and steam for a minute or two, until the eggs are just cooked through but still wobbly.

Divide the rice between serving bowls, then carefully slide the egg and chicken onto the rice. Drizzle each bowl with a few spoonfuls of the sauce and finish with the remaining mitsuba. Serve with shichimi togarashi, if desired.

NOTE: Mitsuba, also known as Japanese wild parsley, can be found in Japanese supermarkets. Alternatively, it can be substituted with spring onion (scallion).

This Korean rice bowl is the perfect dish for summer days when it's too hot to fire up the stove. The vegetables are simply sliced and the salmon served raw. The sauce does require mixing, but if you already have some leftover from Bibimbap (page 18), you can avoid any effort.

RECIPE BY BILLY LAW

SERVES 2

220 g (8 oz) fresh sashimi-grade salmon

steamed short-grain rice, to serve

1 carrot, cut into thin matchsticks

½ cos (romaine) lettuce, finely shredded

¼ red onion, finely sliced

1 spring onion (scallion), finely sliced

toasted sesame seeds, to garnish

Bibim sauce (page 142), to serve

Slice the salmon into 5 mm (¼ in) thick slices, then cover in plastic wrap and refrigerate until ready to serve.

To assemble, divide the rice between two serving bowls. Top with the carrot, lettuce and onion, and then place the salmon in the centre. Garnish with the spring onion and sesame seeds, and serve with bibim sauce on the side.

NOTE: Instead of bibim sauce, you can serve this dish with Spicy soy and spring onion sauce (page 143).

PAD KAPHRAO

In this much loved dish, kaphrao (stir-fried holy basil) is combined with minced (ground) chicken, and a fried egg served on rice. Easily found at street-food stalls in Thailand, the dish requires less effort to prepare in its home country, where holy basil is easily accessible. Holy basil shouldn't be substituted, however, as its spicy, peppery flavour is unique from other varieties: the dish won't taste the same without it.

RECIPE BY SAREEN ROJANAMETIN & JEAN THAMTHANAKORN

SERVES 2

7 garlic cloves

5 red bird's eye chillies

100 ml (3½ fl oz) neutral oil

2 eggs

400 g (14 oz) minced (ground) chicken

2 tbsp fish sauce

1 tbsp oyster sauce

1 tbsp soy sauce

1 tsp caster (superfine) sugar

1 long red chilli, sliced

25 g (¾ cup loosely packed) holy basil leaves

steamed jasmine rice, to serve

DIPPING SAUCE

2 red and green bird's eye chillies, very finely sliced

2 tbsp fish sauce

Using a mortar and pestle, pound the garlic cloves into a coarse paste, then add the bird's eye chillies and pound them a few times to bruise them. If you prefer the stir-fry to be spicy, pound the chillies into a coarse paste. Set aside.

Heat the oil in a wok over medium heat until it begins to smoke. Fry the eggs in the oil until crisp, then remove from the wok with a slotted spoon and set aside to drain on paper towel.

Increase the heat to high. Using the left-over oil, stir-fry the garlic and chilli mixture until fragrant. Add the minced chicken and cook, stirring constantly to break it up, until the chicken is browned and almost cooked all the way through. Pour the fish sauce down the side of the wok, so that it pools beneath the chicken, and allow it to cook undisturbed for 1 minute, until caramelised.

Add the oyster sauce, soy sauce, sugar and long red chilli and stir-fry to combine. Add 75 ml (2½ fl oz) of water to the wok to deglaze, followed by the holy basil leaves. Stir-fry until the basil leaves are just wilted and remove from the heat.

To make the dipping sauce, combine the sliced chilli and the fish sauce.

Serve the pad kaphrao warm with the fried eggs, rice, and the dipping sauce.

Ochazuke is served with tea or dashi to pour over the rice and its accompaniments. Regionally, the toppings vary, options including salmon and umeboshi – this recipe uses both, along with shredded nori. A traditional Japanese dish, ochazuke makes for a light meal on its own or a refreshing last course.

RECIPE BY BILLY LAW

SERVES 1

1 salmon fillet (100 g/ 3½ oz), skin on

2 tsp sencha (or use genmaicha, hojicha or mugicha)

185 g (1 cup) steamed short-grain rice, at room temperature

1 tbsp furikake seasoning (flavour of your choice)

1 umeboshi, pitted

shredded nori, to garnish

toasted white sesame seeds, to garnish

wasabi, to taste

Sprinkle salt generously over the salmon and cure the fillet for 1–2 hours.

Preheat the oven to 200°C (400°F). Wipe the excess salt and moisture off the salmon with paper towel and pat dry. Place the salmon on a wire rack over a baking tray and bake in the oven for 15–20 minutes, until the skin is crispy. Remove from the oven and set aside.

To prepare the tea, put the tea leaves in a teapot. Bring 250 ml (1 cup) of water to the appropriate temperature for your tea, then pour into the teapot and brew the tea for 1–2 minutes.

Stir the furikake into the rice, mixing well, then transfer the rice to a serving bowl. Tear the cured salmon into bite-sized pieces and arrange on top of the rice. Top with the umeboshi, then sprinkle with nori strips and sesame seeds.

When ready to serve, pour the hot tea around the edges of the bowl until the rice is submerged to your liking. Serve with wasabi on the side.

GYUDON

Among the donburi Japan offers, this bowl of finely sliced tender beef and onion really shines. While Gyudon is often thought of as Japan's version of fast food, the bed of rice absorbs the sweet and salty sauce that the toppings are cooked in, creating a comforting dish that's perfect to make at home.

RECIPE BY BILLY LAW

SERVES 2

250 g (9 oz) beef scotch fillet with fat

2 tsp neutral oil

1 onion, finely sliced

3 tbsp soy sauce

3 tbsp mirin

1 tbsp granulated sugar

½ tsp Hondashi (dashi powder; optional)

steamed short-grain rice, to serve

pickled ginger, to garnish

1 spring onion (scallion), finely sliced (optional)

Place the beef in the freezer for 20 minutes.

Holding a knife at a 45-degree angle, cut the beef into thin slices. If the beef starts to thaw and is too soft to slice, put it back in the freezer and repeat the process. Set the slices aside and rest to room temperature.

Heat the oil in a wok over high heat and saute the onion for about 1 minute, until slightly brown. Add 125 ml (½ cup) of water, the soy sauce, mirin, sugar and Hondashi, if using, stir well and bring to a simmer. Reduce the heat to medium and simmer for about 2 minutes, until the onion is soft. Add the beef, spreading it out over the wok, and simmer for 4–5 minutes, skimming off any impurities that float to the surface. Taste and adjust the seasoning accordingly.

Divide the rice between serving bowls and spoon the beef mixture over the rice. Drizzle some sauce on top and finish with pickled ginger and the spring onion, if desired.

HOI AN CHICKEN

Named for the Vietnamese town it comes from, this tender chicken and rice dish is succulent and fresh. The unique mix of ingredients, including turmeric, papaya and tangy pickles, gives Hoi An chicken its distinctive flavour profile.

RECIPE BY JERRY MAI

SERVES 4

1 × 1.8 kg (4 lb) free-range chicken

1 tbsp salt

1 tbsp ground turmeric

400 g (2 cups) jasmine rice

50 g (¼ cup) glutinous rice

Nuoc mam dipping sauce (see page 142), to serve

SALAD

200 g (7 oz) green papaya, shredded

1 onion, finely sliced

1 bunch Vietnamese mint, leaves picked

100 g (3½ oz) Pickled carrot and daikon (see page 144)

Rinse the chicken and pat dry with paper towel. Bring a large saucepan of water to the boil, add the chicken, salt and turmeric and poach the chicken for 15 minutes. Turn off the heat and leave the chicken in the liquid for a further 25 minutes, then remove the chicken and cool on a wire rack. Reserve the poaching liquid.

Combine the jasmine rice and glutinous rice and rinse under cold water for 2 minutes, moving the rice the whole time to ensure each grain is well rinsed. Drain and transfer to a saucepan and pour in enough poaching liquid to cover the rice by about 2 cm (¾ in). Place over medium heat, bring to the boil, then reduce the heat to a simmer and cook for 15 minutes or until the liquid has been absorbed and the rice is tender.

Cut the chicken thighs from the chicken and chop into small pieces. Remove the breast meat from the bone and thickly slice. Place the thighs, chicken breast and wings on a large serving plate.

Combine the salad ingredients in a bowl. Divide the nuoc mam among individual serving bowls.

To serve, spoon the rice onto plates, along with the salad. Invite everyone to help themselves to the poached chicken and add their own nuoc mam.

Khao moo dang is a Chinese-style Thai dish made with char siu, served on a bed of rice. What makes it really special is the gravy that saturates the meat and rice with sweet, rich flavours good enough to make this dish a Thai street-food favourite.

RECIPE BY BILLY LAW

SERVES 4

450 g (1 lb) boneless pork shoulder

2 tbsp oyster sauce

2 tbsp soy sauce

1 tbsp dark soy sauce

2 tbsp granulated sugar

1 tbsp cornflour (corn starch)

4 hard-boiled eggs, peeled

steamed jasmine rice, to serve

1 cucumber, finely sliced

MARINADE

2 tbsp soy sauce

1 tbsp dark soy sauce

2 tsp Chinese five-spice

2 tbsp honey

1 tbsp sesame oil

3 garlic cloves, finely chopped

½ tsp ground white pepper

Cut the pork into long strips 5–7.5 cm (2–3 in) thick and place in a ziplock bag. Add all the marinade ingredients, seal the bag and massage the pork until well coated. Transfer to the fridge to marinate for at least 6 hours, preferably overnight.

Remove the pork from the marinade and place on a wire rack in a roasting tin. Set the marinade aside and let the pork sit until room temperature.

Heat the oven to 200°C (400°F). Transfer the pork with the rack and roasting tin to the oven, then pour about 1 cm (½ in) of hot water into the tin to avoid the drippings from burning. Roast the pork for 20 minutes, then flip and roast for another 20 minutes. Flip the pork again and roast for 10 minutes on each side until caramelised on the edges. Remove from the oven and let rest for 10 minutes.

Meanwhile, make the gravy. Pour the left-over marinade into a saucepan and add the oyster sauce, soy sauces and sugar. Stir and bring to a simmer over medium heat.

Mix the cornflour with 375 ml (1½ cups) of water and pour into the marinade while stirring. Stir until the sauce thickens, then add the eggs and reduce the heat to the lowest setting to keep warm.

When ready to serve, remove the eggs with a slotted spoon and halve them.

Place the rice on a serving plate. Cut the pork into 5 mm (¼ in) thick slices and fan these out over the rice. Drizzle spoonfuls of the gravy over the pork and serve with the eggs and cucumber slices.

VANGI BATH

India's Vangi bath varies, some versions spicier than others, but it's always aromatic and always features vangi (eggplant/aubergine).

RECIPE BY BILLY LAW

SERVES 4

2 Lebanese eggplants (aubergines)

1 tbsp neutral oil

1 tsp mustard seeds

1 tsp cumin seeds

2 tbsp peanuts, skin on

1 tsp urad dal (black gram)

1 tsp chana dal (split chickpeas)

2 green chillies (see Note), split lengthways

1 sprig curry leaves

1 tbsp tamarind paste

½ tsp ground turmeric

1 tsp brown sugar

555 g (3 cups) steamed basmati rice, at room temperature

handful of coriander (cilantro) leaves, chopped

VANGI BATH MASALA

1 cinnamon stick, broken into small pieces

1 tsp cloves

5 cardamom pods

1 mace

2 tsp white poppy seeds

2 tsp neutral oil

10 g (¼ cup) coriander seeds

1 tbsp cumin seeds

1 tsp fenugreek seeds

35 g (½ cup) fresh shredded coconut, water squeezed out

60 g (¼ cup) chana dal

50 g (¼ cup) urad dal

20 (40g) dried Kashmiri red chillies

First make the vangi bath masala. In a frying pan over low heat, roast the cinnamon, cloves, cardamom pods and mace, stirring, for 1 minute or until fragrant. Transfer the spices to a tray to cool, then roast the poppy seeds for 1 minute or until they are slightly golden and start to pop. Transfer to the tray.

Heat 1 teaspoon of the oil in the pan and add the coriander, cumin and fenugreek seeds, the coconut shaves and both dals. Stir and roast until the dals are lightly brown and the coconut is aromatic, then transfer to the tray. Heat the second teaspoon of oil and roast the Kashmiri chillies until puffed up and crispy, then transfer to the tray. Once everything has cooled completely, transfer to a spice grinder or use a mortar and pestle and process into a fine powder. Pour the spice mix into an airtight container.

Cut the eggplants in half, then cut into thick slices. Soak in a bowl of salted water and set aside.

Heat the oil in a large, deep frying-pan over medium heat and add the mustard seeds, cumin seeds, peanuts and both dals. Roast for about a minute, until the peanuts are golden brown. Add the green chillies and curry leaves and stir-fry for another minute.

Drain the eggplant, transfer to the pan and saute for 2 minutes. Mix the tamarind paste with 125 ml (½ cup) of water and add it to the pan, along with the turmeric and ½ teaspoon of salt. Mix well. Cover and simmer for about 5 minutes until the eggplant is soft. Add the brown sugar and 2 tablespoons of the spice mix, stir and cook for about 2 minutes, until the liquid evaporates.

Add the rice and stir until evenly coated. Taste and adjust the seasoning accordingly. Cover, reduce the heat to low and steam the rice for 5 minutes. Uncover and fluff the rice.

To serve, garnish with the coriander.

NOTE: We are using Hari Mirch (Indian green chillies), which are available at any Indian supermarket. They can be substituted with green bird's eye chillies.

The remaining masala can be stored in an airtight container until it loses its fragrance.

Affordable rice dishes are a popular lunch for office workers in Vietnam. Ingredients vary, but often include aromatic pork chops and pork loaf, eggs served sunny side up and a salad for a bite of something fresh. Everything is served atop broken rice, which gives this dish its name – Com tam, or Broken rice.

RECIPE BY JERRY MAI

SERVES 4

4 pork chops

400 g (2 cups) jasmine rice

1 tbsp neutral oil

4 eggs

2 Lebanese (short) cucumbers, sliced diagonally

2 tomatoes, halved and sliced

100 g (3½ oz) Pickled carrot and daikon (see page 144)

4 thick slices Pork loaf (page 147)

80 ml (⅓ cup) Spring onion oil (see page 142)

250 ml (1 cup) Nuoc mam dipping sauce (see page 142)

MARINADE

3 tbsp neutral oil

pinch of ground white pepper

2 tbsp finely chopped lemongrass (white part only)

2 tbsp finely chopped garlic

2 tbsp honey

100 ml (3½ fl oz) fish sauce

1 tbsp caster (superfine) sugar

1 red bird's eye chilli, finely chopped

To marinate the pork chops, combine the marinade ingredients in a large bowl. Tenderise the pork chops by lightly beating them with a meat mallet. Add to the marinade and mix well to coat the chops. Set aside for at least 3 hours or, preferably, overnight.

Rinse the rice under cold water, then cook in a rice cooker according to the manufacturer's instructions.

Prepare a charcoal grill or preheat a grill (broiler) to medium–high. When the charcoal grill is ready (the embers should be glowing red with a small flame on the charcoal), place the pork chops on the grill and cook, frequently turning and basting with the marinade, for 15 minutes or until cooked through.

Heat the oil in a frying pan over medium–high heat. Crack the eggs into the pan and fry sunny side up. Allow the undersides of the eggs to get slightly crispy, then remove and rest on a plate lined with paper towel.

To assemble, spoon the rice onto serving plates and arrange the cucumber, tomato, pickles and a thick slice of pork loaf around the edge. Top with a pork chop and fried egg and drizzle a little spring onion oil over the pork chop. Serve with nuoc mam on the side.

This Singaporean dish can feature different rices, different cooking methods for the duck, and variations in the thickness of the sauce. Here, the duck is braised until tender and served atop jasmine rice.

RECIPE BY BILLY LAW

SERVES 4

10 hard-boiled eggs, peeled

450 g (1 lb) firm tofu

2 tbsp cornflour (corn starch)

steamed jasmine rice, to serve

1 cucumber, sliced diagonally

handful of coriander (cilantro) leaves, chopped (optional)

chilli sauce, to serve

BRAISED DUCK

1 whole duck (1.6 kg/ 3½ lb)

60 ml (¼ cup) neutral oil

10 garlic cloves

100 g (3½ oz) Asian shallots

50 g (1¾ oz) ginger, thickly sliced

50 g (1¾ oz) galangal, thickly sliced

3 cinnamon sticks

5 star anise

1 tbsp cloves

5 dried mandarin peels

1 tbsp black peppercorns

250 ml (1 cup) dark soy sauce

125 ml (½ cup) soy sauce

6 tbsp brown sugar

60 g (2 oz) granulated sugar

2 tsp salt

To prepare the duck, rub salt all over the duck and set aside for 20 minutes. Rinse the duck to wash off the salt and pat dry with paper towel.

Place the duck on a wire rack over the sink. Bring a kettle or saucepan of water to the boil and scald the duck by carefully pouring the water all over it until the skin tightens slightly.

Heat the oil in a wok over medium–low heat. Add the garlic, shallots, ginger and galangal and stir-fry for about 1 minute until fragrant. Add the cinnamon sticks, star anise, cloves, mandarin peels and peppercorns and mix well. Add the soy sauces and reduce the heat to low. Simmer for 2 minutes, then turn off the heat.

Place the duck in a large saucepan in which it is snugly fit and boil more water. Add the spice mixture to the duck and pour the hot water into the pan until the duck is almost fully submerged. Add the sugars and salt and bring to the boil over high heat. Once boiling, reduce the heat to low, cover and braise the duck for 1½ hours, turning the duck over after 1 hour. Once cooked, transfer the duck to a tray and let rest for 30 minutes.

Strain 2 litres (2 qts) of the braising stock into another large pan and discard the solids. Bring the stock to a simmer over low heat, taste and adjust the seasoning accordingly. Add the eggs and tofu and braise for 30 minutes. Remove the eggs and tofu and set aside.

Mix the cornflour with 125 ml (½ cup) of water to make a slurry. Increase the heat to medium and pour the slurry into the stock in a steady stream while stirring at the same time until it thickens, about 1 minute.

Chop up the duck into bite-sized pieces, halve the eggs and cut the tofu into slices.

Divide the rice between serving plates and top with a few pieces of the braised duck. Pour a ladleful of gravy over the duck and rice and garnish with the cucumber and coriander, if desired. Serve the egg halves, tofu slices and chilli sauce on the side.

SINGAPORE DUCK RICE

Serving this rice in a pineapple isn't necessary, but it makes for an impressive-looking dish. Bursting with bright flavour from the chunks of fruit mixed in, the sweetness in Pineapple fried rice is balanced by the savoury ingredients, which are at their best when the rice is made the day before, as with any fried rice.

RECIPE BY SAREEN ROJANAMETIN & JEAN THAMTHANAKORN

SERVES 2

80 ml (⅓ cup) neutral oil

2 garlic cloves, finely chopped

500 g (1 lb 2 oz) banana prawns (shrimp), peeled and deveined

1 Asian shallot, diced

400 g (14 oz) steamed jasmine rice, refrigerated overnight

1 tbsp soy sauce

1 tbsp oyster sauce

1 tbsp fish sauce

1 tsp caster (superfine) sugar

170 g (6 oz) fresh pineapple, cut into 2 cm (¾ in) cubes

1 spring onion (scallion), finely sliced

60 g (2 oz) roasted cashews

1 tbsp coriander (cilantro) leaves

2 lime wedges

Heat the oil in a wok over medium heat and stir-fry the garlic until fragrant. Increase the heat to high and add the prawns and shallot, stir-frying until the prawns are just cooked through.

Add the rice to the wok and stir-fry for 1–2 minutes, until the rice is well coated with oil. Season with the soy sauce, oyster sauce, fish sauce and sugar and stir-fry for 2–3 minutes. Add the pineapple, spring onion and cashews and stir-fry for a further 1–2 minutes, until well combined. Remove from the heat and transfer to a serving bowl or a hollowed-out pineapple half.

To serve, scatter over coriander and accompany with the lime wedges.

Named for its appearance, Golden fried rice takes on colour from the egg yolks that are mixed through the rice. This Chinese technique coats the grains and imparts an aromatic flavour that pairs well with a simple mix of additions. Here we keep things basic with spring onions (scallions) and garlic. Feel free to tweak the ingredients but make sure to avoid moisture-heavy options.

RECIPE BY BILLY LAW

SERVES 2

370 g (2 cups) steamed jasmine rice, refrigerated overnight, at room temperature

4 egg yolks

2 tbsp neutral oil

2 spring onions (scallions), cut into 10 cm (4 in) lengths, plus finely sliced spring onion to serve

5 garlic cloves, left whole or finely sliced

1 tsp salt

Add the rice and yolks to a large bowl. Use a rice paddle to separate clumps and mix until every grain is well coated.

Heat the oil in a wok over medium–high heat and add the spring onion and garlic, stir-frying for about 2 minutes until fragrant and golden brown. Drain the oil through a fine-mesh sieve into a heatproof bowl, leaving just a little oil in the wok. Set the garlic aside and discard the spring onion.

Heat the same wok over high heat until it starts to smoke. Add the rice and stir-fry for 1–2 minutes until the rice is dry and dances in the wok. Add the salt and 1 tablespoon of the reserved garlic oil and stir-fry for 15 seconds. Turn off the heat, add the fresh spring onion and give it a quick stir, then transfer the fried rice to a serving plate. Garnish with the garlic.

TAPSILOG

A popular choice for breakfast in the Philippines. Like any silog, this dish pairs garlic fried rice, a fried egg and a protein. The 'tap' in the name refers to 'tapa', or beef. While the beef in this dish was traditionally cured, it's now commonly marinated and then grilled or fried, as in this recipe.

RECIPE BY BILLY LAW

SERVES 4

125 ml (½ cup) neutral oil

12 garlic cloves, finely chopped

4 large eggs

740 g (4 cups) steamed jasmine rice, refrigerated overnight, at room temperature

soy sauce, to taste

GRILLED BEEF

450 g (1 lb) beef sirloin, cut into thin strips

6 garlic cloves, finely chopped

2 tbsp soy sauce

2 tbsp kecap manis (see Note)

1 tbsp white vinegar

2 tsp cornflour (corn starch)

1 tsp chilli flakes

½ tsp freshly ground black pepper

pinch of salt, to taste

Prepare the beef by mixing all the ingredients in a bowl. Cover and marinate in the fridge for at least 6 hours, preferably overnight, then bring to room temperature.

Heat the oil in a saucepan over medium–low heat. Add the garlic and fry, stirring occasionally, for about 5 minutes, until golden brown and crisp. Drain the garlic oil through a fine-mesh sieve into a heatproof bowl and transfer the garlic crisps to a small bowl. Set aside.

Heat 2 tablespoons of the garlic oil in a wok over high heat. Spread half of the beef evenly over the wok and cook for about 1 minute until slightly charred, then flip over and cook for another minute. Transfer to a plate and repeat with the remaining beef. Set aside and keep warm.

Wipe the wok clean and heat 2 tablespoons of the garlic oil over medium–high heat. Add the rice, breaking up any clumps, and stir until the rice is well coated in garlic oil. Cook for about 3 minutes, until the rice is dry and dancing in the wok. Add half of the garlic crisps and mix well, then transfer the rice to a bowl and keep warm.

Wipe the wok clean and heat 2 tablespoons of the garlic oil over medium heat. Fry the eggs for about 2 minutes without flipping, until the whites are almost set and the yolks are still runny.

Transfer the rice to serving plates and top with the beef strips and eggs. Garnish with the remaining garlic crisps, and finish with a dash of soy sauce.

NOTE: Kecap manis is a popular Indonesian ingredient. With the rich consistency of molasses, it's created with palm sugar and soy sauce, and can be found in most supermarkets.

This gem from Laotian kitchens is made by creating rice balls that are crumbled and mixed into an aromatic salad bursting with citrus, herbs and bites of pork sausage. The list of ingredients isn't short, but the time it takes to prepare this salad is definitely worth each deliciously crunchy, chewy bite.

RECIPE BY BILLY LAW

SERVES 4

370 g (2 cups) steamed jasmine rice, cooled to room temperature

85 g (1 cup) fresh shredded coconut, water squeezed out

3 tbsp Thai red curry paste

2 tbsp fish sauce

1 tbsp granulated sugar

3 large eggs

2 tbsp cornflour (corn starch)

neutral oil, for deep-frying

2–3 som moo (fermented pork sausages; see Note)

3 makrut lime leaves, finely shredded

80 g (½ cup) roasted peanuts, roughly chopped

3 spring onions (scallions), finely chopped

handful of coriander (cilantro) leaves, roughly chopped

juice of 1 lime

pinch of salt

2–3 cos (romaine) lettuce heads, separated into leaves

Place the rice in a large mixing bowl and add the coconut, curry paste, fish sauce, sugar and 1 egg. Using both hands, gently mix everything together until the rice is evenly coated.

Grab a handful of rice and roll it into a golf ball-sized ball. Repeat with the remaining rice mixture.

Set up a frying station. Beat the remaining eggs in a shallow bowl and place the cornflour on a plate. Fill a large saucepan or wok one-third full with oil and heat to 180°C (350°F); a cube of bread dropped in the oil will brown in 15 seconds.

Roll the rice balls in the cornflour, dust off any excess, then dip in the beaten egg until evenly coated. In small batches, deep-fry the balls for 3–4 minutes until golden brown. Drain on plates lined with paper towels and let cool.

To make the salad, tear up the rice balls and sausages into small pieces and place in a large mixing bowl. Add the lime leaves, peanuts, spring onion, coriander, lime juice and salt and toss everything together until well combined.

Serve the salad in lettuce cups.

NOTE: Som moo is a fermented pork sausage popular in Laos. Known for its sour notes, its flavour is balanced by the chillies and garlic the sausage is prepared with. Som moo is available in Asian supermarkets .

KIMCHI BOKKEUM BAP

If you have a well-stocked pantry, you may not even need to go grocery shopping to make Kimchi fried rice. Although packed with flavour, this Korean dish doesn't need much more than kimchi and gochujang (Korean chilli paste), with a fried egg served on top for a low-effort but tasty meal.

RECIPE BY BILLY LAW

SERVES 2

2 tbsp neutral oil

2 garlic cloves, crushed

150 g (1 cup) cabbage kimchi, roughly chopped

500 g (2⅔ cups) steamed short-grain rice, refrigerated overnight, at room temperature

60 ml (¼ cup) kimchi juice

2 tbsp gochujang (Korean chilli paste)

2 tsp sesame oil

1 spring onion (scallion), finely sliced

2 fried eggs, sunny side up, to serve

Heat the oil in a wok over medium–high heat. Add the garlic and stir-fry for 1 minute until fragrant. Add the kimchi and stir-fry for another minute.

Add the rice, breaking up any clumps. Add the kimchi juice and gochujang and stir-fry for 3–4 minutes until well combined. Reduce the heat if the rice begins to stick to the bottom of the pan.

Add the sesame oil and season with salt and pepper to taste. Add half the spring onion, mix well, then divide the fried rice between serving bowls. Garnish with the remaining spring onion and top each bowl with a fried egg. Serve immediately.

NOTE: You can also make a fancy version of this kimchi fried rice by adding thin slices of pork belly, bacon or even SPAM.

YEUNG CHAU CHOW FAN

A classic serve of this Hong Kong-style fried rice is so delicious, it can be found in Chinese restaurants around the world.

RECIPE BY ARCHAN CHAN

SERVES 2–3

3 tbsp neutral oil

2 eggs, lightly beaten

555 g (3 cups) steamed jasmine rice, refrigerated overnight

100 g (3½ oz) small prawns (shrimp), peeled and deveined

100 g (3½ oz) choy sum stem (Chinese flowering cabbage), sliced

finely sliced spring onion (scallion), to garnish

CHAR SIU

500 g (1 lb 2 oz) boneless pork collar, cut lengthways into 4 pieces

30 g (¼ cup) cornflour (corn starch)

250 g (9 oz) honey

MARINADE

100 g (3½ oz) caster (superfine) sugar

1 tbsp fine sea salt

2 tbsp hoisin sauce

2 tbsp oyster sauce

2 tsp sesame paste

1 tsp soy sauce

1 tsp dark soy sauce

½ tsp finely chopped Asian shallot

1 tsp grated garlic

1 tbsp rose wine

1 egg, lightly beaten

SAUCE

40 g (1½ oz) soft brown sugar

1 tbsp soy sauce

120 g (4½ oz) warm honey

2 tsp fine sea salt

To prepare the char siu, soak the pork in slightly salted water (about 1 teaspoon of salt for every 1 litre/1 qt) for 15 minutes. Drain and toss the pork with 20 g (¾ oz) of the cornflour, then wrap in plastic wrap and marinate in the fridge for 4 hours. Rinse off the cornflour and pat dry, then toss the pork in the remaining cornflour to coat well.

To make the marinade, mix the ingredients in a large bowl. Add the pork and turn to coat well, then cover and marinate in the fridge for 1 hour.

Preheat the oven to 240°C (465°F). Line a baking tray with foil. Spread the pork out on the tray and roast for 5 minutes. Turn the pork over and roast for another 5 minutes. Reduce the temperature to 100°C (210°F) and roast for 30 minutes. Remove the pork and turn the oven back up to 240°C.

Brush both sides of the pork with the honey. Return to the oven and roast for 5 minutes, or until the honey is bubbling and caramelising. Turn the pork over and cook for another 5 minutes. Reduce the temperature to 100°C (210°F) and roast for a further 30 minutes. Remove from the oven and brush with honey again.

Meanwhile, to make the sauce, combine the ingredients with 3 tablespoons of water in a saucepan. Bring to a simmer over low heat, then remove from the heat.

Cut the char siu into 1 cm (½ in) pieces and pour the sauce over the top. Reserve 100 g (3½ oz) and transfer the rest to an airtight container. The char siu will keep in the fridge for up to 3 days – reheat before serving.

Heat a large wok over high until very hot. Turn off the heat, add 2 tablespoons of the oil, then quickly add the egg and cook for about 10 seconds. Turn the heat back on, add the rice and stir-fry to evenly distribute the egg, then lightly press it flat against the wok. Cook for 2 minutes until some of the moisture has evaporated, but the rice is not too dry.

Heat the remaining oil in a second wok over high heat, add the prawns and choy sum and stir-fry for 1 minute. Add the prawns, choy sum and char siu to the rice and stir-fry for 1 minute. Finish with the spring onion and serve immediately.

In Malaysia, nasi goreng, or fried rice, is a broad and beloved category. Some are similar to fried rices from other countries, but Nasi goreng kampung is a staple that stands out thanks to its use of distinct ingredients, including belacan and anchovies. Sweet and salty, there's little question why this is a favourite in its home country.

RECIPE BY AIM ARIS & AHMAD SALIM

SERVES 4

90 ml (3 fl oz) neutral oil

4 eggs

200 g (7 oz) boneless, skinless chicken breast, cut into small pieces

90 g (¾ cup) finely sliced snake (yard-long) beans

1 large handful of kangkung (water spinach)

2 tbsp oyster sauce

740 g (4 cups) steamed long-grain or basmati rice, refrigerated overnight

crispy fried anchovies, to garnish (optional)

FRIED RICE PASTE

1 onion

2 Asian shallots

3 garlic cloves

6–8 red or green bird's eye chillies

1 tsp toasted belacan (shrimp paste; optional)

2 tbsp dried anchovies

To make the fried rice paste, use a mortar and pestle to pound all the ingredients until they form a coarse paste; you can also use a small food processor or blender. Set aside.

Heat 2 tablespoons of the oil in a wok over medium heat and add an egg. Cook until the top of the white is set but the yolk is still runny. Remove the egg with a spatula and cook the remaining eggs, one at a time.

Heat the remaining oil the wok over medium heat. Add the fried rice paste and saute for 1–2 minutes until aromatic. Add the chicken and cook for 1 minute.

Add the snake beans and saute for 15 seconds, followed by the kangkung. Stir to combine, then add the oyster sauce.

Add the rice and toss everything together over high heat for 1 minute. Season to taste with salt and continue stirring until the rice is toasted and the chicken is cooked through.

Immediately serve the fried rice with the eggs and crispy fried anchovies, if desired.

KHAO PAD PU

Thailand's crab fried rice is simple, with little more added than tender, sweet chunks of crabmeat and rich bites of egg. However, that doesn't mean it lacks in flavour: this easy-to-make dish is a favourite in Thailand, where it's popular dining in or out.

RECIPE BY SAREEN ROJANAMETIN & JEAN THAMTHANAKORN

SERVES 2

80 ml (⅓ cup) neutral oil

2 garlic cloves, finely chopped

1 egg

400 g (14 oz) steamed jasmine rice, refrigerated overnight

1 tbsp soy sauce

1 tbsp oyster sauce

1 tbsp fish sauce

1 tsp caster (superfine) sugar

½ tsp ground white pepper

2 spring onions (scallions), finely sliced

200 g (7 oz) cooked crabmeat

1 tbsp shredded coriander (cilantro) leaves

Heat the oil in a wok over high heat until it begins to shimmer. Add the garlic and stir-fry until fragrant and beginning to brown.

Crack the egg into the oil and allow it to firm up a little before stirring to break it up. Add the rice, reduce the heat to medium and stir-fry for 1–2 minutes, until the rice is well coated in the oil and the egg is distributed evenly. Season with the soy sauce, oyster sauce, fish sauce, sugar and white pepper, then add the spring onion and stir gently to combine.

Mix in almost all of the crabmeat, setting aside a little for garnishing. Remove from the heat and transfer to a serving bowl.

Just before serving, sprinkle with the coriander leaves and reserved crabmeat.

PULIHORA

For lovers of zestier recipes, Pulihora is a tamarind rice from Andhra Pradesh in India that's prepared for family meals, as well as festive occasions and as an offering at temples. The sourness from the tamarind is mixed with heat and salt for a balanced depth of flavour.

RECIPE BY BILLY LAW

SERVES 4

125 ml (½ cup) neutral oil

½ tsp mustard seeds

½ tsp cumin seeds

40 g (¼ cup) raw peanuts, skin on

40 g (¼ cup) raw cashews

2 tsp chana dal (split chickpeas)

2 tsp urad dal (black gram)

1 tsp ground turmeric

2 sprigs curry leaves

2–4 green chillies (see Note), split lengthways

5–6 dried Kashmiri red chillies

2 tbsp tamarind paste

1 tsp salt

555 g (3 cups) steamed basmati rice, at room temperature

85 g (½ cup) tinned chickpeas (optional)

Heat the oil in a large frying pan over low heat. Add the mustard and cumin seeds and the peanuts, and stir-fry for about 1 minute until fragrant and the peanuts are roasted.

Add the cashews and stir-fry for another minute. Add both dals, the turmeric, curry leaves and green chillies and stir-fry for 30 seconds. Add the Kashmiri chillies and stir-fry for a further 30 seconds.

Add the tamarind paste, salt and 60 ml (¼ cup) of water. Increase the heat to medium and mix well. Cook for 3–5 minutes, until the liquid has reduced and thickened.

Add the rice and chickpeas, if using, stirring until evenly coated and warm.

NOTE: We are using Hari Mirch (Indian green chillies), which are available at any Indian supermarket. They can be substituted with green bird's eyes chillies.

Introduced by China, mustard greens are a popular ingredient for pickling in Japan. The pickles, or takana, are delicious added to a range of recipes, including Chinese-style fried rice (chahan). Like many Japanese dishes, Takana chahan is simple but flavourful, combining only a few ingredients to great effect.

RECIPE BY BILLY LAW

SERVES 2

370 g (2 cups) steamed short-grain rice, refrigerated overnight, at room temperature

2 tbsp neutral oil

2 large eggs, beaten with a pinch of salt

1 tbsp sesame oil

120 g (4½ oz) takana (pickled mustard green), chopped

1 spring onion (scallion), white part only, finely sliced

½ tsp salt

2 tsp soy sauce

pinch of ground white pepper, to taste

½ tsp Hondashi (dashi powder; optional)

Tip the rice into a bowl and break up any clumps.

Heat a wok over high heat until just smoking, then add the oil and swirl around to coat the wok evenly. Reduce the heat to medium–high and add the egg, scrambling until just cooked. Remove from the wok and set aside.

Add the sesame oil and takana to the wok and stir-fry for 30 seconds, or until the liquid has evaporated. Add the rice and egg, and stir-fry for a few minutes, breaking the egg into smaller pieces and tossing the wok occasionally, until the rice dances in the wok. Add the spring onion, salt, soy sauce, white pepper and Hondashi, if using, then stir-fry for another minute until well mixed.

Transfer to a plate and serve.

TAKANA CHAHAN

This dim sum classic features glutinous rice that's both fried and steamed. The grain's chewiness, paired with umami-packed pork sausages, dried shrimp and shiitake mushrooms, creates a dish that makes it hard to stop at just one serve.

RECIPE BY BILLY LAW

NUO MI FAN

SERVES 6–8

400 g (2 cups) glutinous rice

5 dried shiitake mushrooms

2 tbsp neutral oil

3 French shallots, finely sliced

3 lap cheong (Chinese sausages), cut diagonally into 5 mm (¼ in) slices

3 tbsp dried shrimp

3 garlic cloves, finely chopped

1 spring onion (scallion), finely sliced

SEASONING

2 tbsp soy sauce

1½ tbsp dark soy sauce

1 tbsp oyster sauce

60 ml (¼ cup) Shaoxing rice wine

1 tbsp granulated sugar

2 tsp sesame oil

½ tsp ground white pepper

Wash the rice until the water runs clear, then transfer to a bowl and add enough water to cover the rice by at least 2.5 cm (1 in). Soak for at least 6 hours. Drain and set aside.

Soak the mushrooms in boiling water for about 30 minutes until fully rehydrated. Squeeze the mushrooms to remove excess water, then cut into thin slices.

Meanwhile, to make the seasoning, add all the ingredients to a bowl, mix well and set aside.

Heat the oil in a wok over medium–low heat, add the shallot and stir-fry for about 5 minutes until crispy and golden brown. Remove from the wok and set aside.

Increase the heat to medium and add the lap cheong to the same pan. Stir-fry for 1 minute to render some of the fat, then add the mushroom and dried shrimp and stir-fry for a further minute. Add the garlic and fried shallot and stir-fry for 1 minute, then pour in the seasoning. Stir for about 1 minute to combine and reduce the sauce slightly. Add the rice and stir for about 2 minutes, until it absorbs all the seasoning.

Meanwhile, over medium–high heat, fill a wok or large saucepan one–third with water and bring to a simmer.

Transfer the rice mixture to a shallow bowl, spreading it evenly. Place the bowl inside a bamboo steamer, cover with the lid and place inside the wok. Steam the rice for 40–50 minutes until fully cooked.

Remove from the heat and let rest for 5 minutes, then fluff the rice. Garnish with the spring onion and serve hot.

HOKKIEN FRIED RICE

This Fujian fried rice marries land and sea. What sets the dish apart isn't what goes in, though. It's what's ladled on top: a rich sauce.

RECIPE BY BILLY LAW

SERVES 6–8

4 small dried shiitake mushrooms

8–10 dried scallops

1½ tbsp neutral oil

2 French shallots, finely chopped

2 garlic cloves, finely chopped

100 g (3½ oz) prawns (shrimp), peeled and deveined, cut into 1 cm (½ in) cubes

80 g (½ cup) frozen peas and diced carrots

1 tbsp cornflour (corn starch)

CHICKEN

200 g (7 oz) boneless, skinless chicken thigh, diced into 1 cm (½ in) cubes

1 tbsp oyster sauce

1 tsp neutral oil

1 tsp cornflour

SAUCE BASE

2 tbsp oyster sauce

1 tbsp soy sauce

2 tsp dark soy sauce

1 tsp sesame oil

2 tsp granulated sugar

pinch of ground white pepper, to taste

EGG FRIED RICE

1 tbsp neutral oil

2 large eggs, beaten

740 g (4 cups) steamed jasmine rice, refrigerated overnight, at room temperature

2 tsp soy sauce

pinch of ground white pepper, to taste

In boiling water, soak the mushrooms for about 30 minutes until fully rehydrated. Squeeze the mushrooms to remove excess water, dice and set aside. Reserve 375 ml (1½ cups) of the soaking water.

Meanwhile, soak the dried scallops in boiling water for about 30 minutes until softened. Tear the rehydrated scallops into small pieces and set aside.

To prepare the chicken, mix the chicken, oyster sauce, oil and cornflour in a bowl. Set aside to marinate.

Meanwhile, combine all the sauce base ingredients with the reserved mushroom soaking water.

To make the egg fried rice, heat a wok over high heat until just smoking, then reduce the heat to medium. Add the oil and swirl around to coat the wok evenly. Add the egg and scramble for about 30 seconds until cooked. Increase the heat to high and quickly add the rice. Break up any big clumps and stir-fry for about 2 minutes until the rice is dry and dances in the wok. Add the soy sauce, white pepper and ½ teaspoon of salt and stir-fry for another minute, then transfer to a large serving plate.

Heat ½ tablespoon of the oil in the same wok over high heat. Add the marinated chicken, spreading the cubes out evenly, and brown for 30 seconds. Stir-fry for 1 minute or until evenly cooked, then transfer to a bowl and wipe the wok clean.

Heat the remaining oil in the same wok over medium–high heat. Add the scallops and stir-fry for 15–20 seconds until fragrant. Add the mushroom and stir-fry for another 20 seconds, then add the shallot, garlic and prawns, stir-frying for about 30 seconds until the prawns are just cooked through. Return the chicken to the wok, add the peas and carrots, and stir to combine.

Give the sauce base a stir and pour into the wok. Stir everything together and bring to a simmer. Mix the cornflour with 2 tablespoons of water to make a slurry and pour into the wok, stirring continuously until the sauce thickens.

Pour the sauce over the fried rice and serve immediately.

Originating in India's south, curd rice is a favourite throughout the country. Popular to serve at the end of meals, this creamy, healthy dish is made by combining rice and yoghurt, which is then spiced and garnished with toppings such as pomegranate.

RECIPE BY BILLY LAW

SERVES 6-8

555 g (3 cups) steamed basmati rice, refrigerated overnight

500 g (2 cups) plain yoghurt

2 tbsp heavy (double) cream

1 tsp salt

2 tbsp full-cream (whole) milk

2 green chillies (see Note), finely chopped

1 tsp finely chopped ginger

2 tbsp coriander (cilantro) leaves, finely chopped, plus extra to garnish

2 tbsp ghee

10 raw cashews, halved

1 tsp mustard seeds

1 tsp urad dal (black gram)

1 tsp cumin seeds

1 dried red chilli, torn into small pieces

1 sprig curry leaves

pinch of hing (asafoetida)

2 tbsp pomegranate seeds

In a large bowl, break any big clumps of rice and stir to separate the grains.

Add the yoghurt, cream and salt and stir until the rice is evenly coated and slightly mushy. Add the milk and stir until the rice is creamy.

Add the green chillies, ginger and coriander and mix well, then set aside.

Heat the ghee in a small saucepan over medium–low heat. Add the cashews and fry for about 30 seconds until golden. Add the mustard seeds, dal, cumin seeds, chilli, curry leaves and hing and fry for 15 seconds. Pour everything over the curd rice and mix well.

Divide between serving bowls and garnish with the pomegranate seeds and coriander.

NOTE: We are using Hari Mirch (Indian green chillies), which are available at any Indian supermarket. They can be substituted with green bird's eye chillies.

KHAO TOM

Khao tom is a flavourful and aromatic Thai rice soup, which commonly features seafood. Here, barramundi is used for a fresh, light flavour. Like Jok (page 90), this is a common dish in Thailand to enjoy over breakfast.

RECIPE BY SAREEN ROJANAMETIN & JEAN THAMTHANAKORN

SERVES 3

450 ml (15 fl oz) pork stock

1 small whole barramundi, cleaned, filleted and cut into 3–4 cm (1¼–1½ in) slices, bones reserved

250 g (9 oz) steamed jasmine rice

3 tbsp grapeseed oil

2 garlic cloves, roughly chopped

1 tbsp fish sauce

1 tsp soy sauce

1 tsp ground white pepper

1 tbsp Tianjin preserved vegetable (see Note), roughly chopped

5 g (¼ cup) celery leaves, finely chopped

1 spring onion (scallion), finely sliced

10 g (⅓ oz) young ginger, peeled and julienned

In a large saucepan over high heat, bring the pork stock and 350 ml (12 fl oz) of water to the boil. Add the barramundi bones and boil for 5 minutes, then strain the stock through a fine-mesh sieve into a large container. Discard the bones and clean the saucepan.

Add the rice to the clean saucepan along with three-quarters of the stock. Cook over medium–low heat until the rice is tender.

Heat the grapeseed oil in a non-stick frying pan over medium heat and fry the garlic for about 5 minutes until golden and crispy. Using a slotted spoon, remove the garlic crisps from the oil and set aside.

Pan-fry the sliced barramundi in the left-over oil until just cooked through, then add the fish sauce, soy sauce and white pepper. Add the remaining stock to the pan, along with the Tianjin preserved vegetable, and cook for 2 minutes. Transfer the fish and its cooking liquid to the saucepan of rice and gently stir to combine.

Ladle the khao tom into three serving bowls and garnish with the garlic crisps, celery leaves, spring onion and young ginger.

NOTE: Tianjin preserved vegetable is a kind of pickled cabbage from the city of Tianjin in China. Jars of Tianjin preserved vegetable can be found in Asian supermarkets.

CHICKEN BIRYANI

In this biryani, chicken is cooked in a vibrant blend of aromatic spices that permeate the dish, served with bright spoons of rice.

RECIPE BY BILLY LAW

SERVES 4–6

1 kg (2 lb 3 oz) mixed chicken thighs and drumsticks, bone in and skin on

400 g (2 cups) basmati rice

3 tbsp neutral oil

15 g (½ oz) butter

100 g (3½ oz) Asian shallots, thinly sliced

4 dried bay leaves

6 green cardamom pods

1 tsp caraway seeds

8 cloves

2 cinnamon sticks

½ tsp cumin seeds

2 tbsp biryani masala

200 g (1 cup) diced tomatoes

5–6 small green chillies, split lengthways (see Note on page 77)

90 g (3 oz) plain yoghurt

10–12 saffron threads

2 tbsp warm milk

15 g (½ cup) coriander (cilantro) leaves

raita, to serve

CHICKEN MARINADE

1 tbsp grated ginger

1 tbsp grated garlic

½ tsp ground turmeric

1 tsp ground red chilli

1 tsp ground coriander

Make a few incisions on each piece of chicken and place in a large bowl. Add the chicken marinade ingredients and 2 teaspoons of salt and mix well. Cover and marinate in the fridge for at least 2 hours, but preferably overnight.

Wash the rice until the water runs clear, then soak in a bowl of water for 30 minutes. Drain and set aside.

Heat the oil and butter in a large saucepan over medium heat. Saute the shallot for about 3 minutes until golden brown. Add 2 of the bay leaves, 3 cardamom pods, half the caraway seeds, 4 cloves, 1 cinnamon stick and the cumin seeds and stir-fry for about 1 minute until fragrant.

Add the marinated chicken and cook for about 5 minutes, stirring now and then, until lightly brown all over. Add the biryani masala and mix well for another minute, then add the tomato and cook for about 1 minute until softened. Add the green chillies and stir for 15 seconds, then add the yoghurt and 60 ml (¼ cup) of water and stir until combined, scraping the bottom of the pan to dislodge any caramelised bits. Cover and cook the chicken for 20 minutes.

Bring a large saucepan of water to a rolling boil over medium–high heat. Add 2 teaspoons of salt, the remaining caraway seeds, cinnamon stick, cloves, bay leaves and cardamom pods and simmer for 3 minutes. Scoop out the seasonings and discard. Add the rice to the seasoned water, reduce the heat to medium and simmer for 6–8 minutes, until the rice is par-cooked. Drain the rice and set aside.

Taste the chicken and adjust the seasoning accordingly. If there is a lot of sauce in the pan, uncover and continue to cook until almost all the sauce has evaporated, leaving only a few spoonfuls at the bottom of the pan.

In a small bowl, stir the saffron into the warm milk and set aside to infuse for 5 minutes.

Reduce the heat to the lowest setting and cover the chicken with the rice. Scatter most of the coriander leaves over the top, then drizzle with the saffron-infused milk. Put the lid back on and steam the rice for 20 minutes.

Turn off the heat and let the biryani rest for 10 minutes, then fluff the rice but do not overmix. Garnish with the remaining coriander and serve with raita on the side.

Like Chinese congee, Filipino lugaw is a hearty dish of rice cooked until it takes on a creamy consistency. Arroz caldo adds chicken and is prepared with aromatics and fish sauce. Finished with an array of toppings, including hard-boiled eggs and toasted garlic, it's a comforting way to start the morning.

RECIPE BY BILLY LAW

SERVES 4–6

60 ml (¼ cup) neutral oil

10 garlic cloves, finely chopped

1 onion, finely sliced

500 g (1 lb 2 oz) boneless, skinless chicken thighs, sliced into bite-sized pieces

1 tbsp grated ginger

1 tbsp fish sauce

1 tsp freshly ground black pepper, to taste

6 cups low- or no-sodium chicken stock

200 g (1 cup) jasmine rice

2 hard-boiled eggs, halved

2 spring onions (scallions), finely sliced

4 lime wedges

Heat the oil in a pan over medium–low heat. Add the garlic and fry for about 5 minutes until golden and crispy. Drain the garlic oil through a fine-mesh sieve into a heatproof bowl and transfer the garlic crisps to a small bowl. Set aside.

Heat 2 tablespoons of the garlic oil in a large stockpot over medium–high heat and add the onion. Saute for about 1 minute until softened and translucent. Add the chicken and cook for about 3 minutes until browned. Add the ginger, fish sauce, black pepper and half the garlic crisps, mixing well.

Pour in the chicken stock and rice and increase the heat to high. Sir and scrape the bottom of the pot to dislodge any caramelised bits. Bring to the boil, then reduce the heat to low, cover and simmer, stirring occasionally, for about 30 minutes, until the rice is a thick porridge, or longer if you like a mushier consistency. Season with salt and pepper to taste.

Divide the porridge among serving bowls and top with the eggs. Garnish with the spring onion and garlic crisps and serve with the lime wedges.

KHICHDI

Moong dal (skinned split mung beans) and rice are cooked together until soft to create Khichdi. The end texture and taste varies, with some versions more porridge-like, some firmer, some heavily spiced, and some kept simple with nothing more than ghee, cumin and turmeric. This version adds more spices and vegetables for a fuller flavour.

RECIPE BY BILLY LAW

SERVES 6–8

300 g (1½ cups) basmati rice

210 g (1 cup) moong dal (skinned split mung beans)

1 tbsp ghee or neutral oil

1 tsp cumin seeds

1 tsp mustard seeds

½ onion, finely chopped

½ tbsp grated ginger

2 green chillies (see Note), finely chopped

2 large tomatoes, diced

155 g (1 cup) frozen green peas

1 tsp ground turmeric

2 tsp salt

1 tsp garam masala

papadums, to serve

roughly chopped coriander (cilantro) leaves, to garnish

Place the rice and dal in a bowl and add enough water to cover everything by at least 2.5 cm (1 in). Soak for 30 minutes, then drain and set aside.

Heat the ghee in a Dutch oven over medium heat and add the cumin and mustard seeds, cooking for about 20 seconds until fragrant. Add the onion and saute for about 1 minute until softened and translucent. Add the ginger and chilli and saute for another minute. Add the tomato and cook for about 2 minutes until softened.

Add the peas and soaked rice and dal, mixing well. Add the turmeric, salt and garam masala, stirring until everything is well coated.

Add 1.5 litres (1½ qts) of water to the Dutch oven and increase the heat to high. Mix well and bring to the boil. Reduce the heat to low, cover and cook for 15–20 minutes, stirring occasionally, until the rice and dal are soft and mushy. If it gets too dry, add water to the desired consistency. Season with salt to taste.

Cook the papadums according to the instructions on the packet.

Divide the khichdi between serving bowls, garnish with coriander and serve with the papadums.

NOTE: We are using Hari Mirch (Indian green chillies), which are available at any Indian supermarket. They can be substituted with green bird's eye chillies.

SAN GWAN JUK

While congee is ubiquitous throughout Asia, the cooking methods and ingredients vary. This recipe hails from Hong Kong and, typical of congee from the area, the ingredients are stir-fried over high heat before they finish cooking in the congee. This comforting and flavourful version features white fish.

RECIPE BY ARCHAN CHAN

SERVES 4

100 g (½ cup) jasmine rice

200 g (7 oz) white fish fillet, such as cod, whiting or barramundi, patted dry and thickly sliced

½ tsp ground white pepper

1 tbsp soy sauce

1 tbsp cornflour (corn starch)

125 ml (½ cup) chicken stock or water

1 tbsp neutral oil

1 tsp finely sliced ginger

1 tbsp Shaoxing rice wine

finely sliced spring onion (scallion), to serve

coriander (cilantro) leaves, to serve

chilli oil, to serve (optional)

Rinse the rice one or twice, then drain and put in the freezer for at least 8 hours. (If you don't have time, you can skip this step but it reduces the cooking time and results in a silkier texture.)

Combine the rice and 2.5 litres (2½ qts) of water in a large saucepan and bring to the boil over high heat, stirring constantly to prevent the rice from sticking to the bottom of the pan. Reduce the heat and simmer for 1 hour or until the rice has broken down and the congee has thickened, stirring occasionally to prevent sticking. (If the rice hasn't been in the freezer, the cooking time will be about 3 hours.)

Place the fish, white pepper, soy sauce and cornflour in a medium bowl and toss together well. Cover and leave to marinate in the fridge for 30 minutes.

Heat 500 ml (2 cups) of the congee and the stock in a saucepan over medium heat; the left-over congee will keep in an airtight container in the fridge for up to 5 days.

Meanwhile, heat the oil in a saucepan (preferably non-stick) over high heat and add the ginger and fish in a single layer. Leave the fish undisturbed for about 30 seconds, then add the Shaoxing wine. Pour in the congee mixture and bring to the boil to cook the fish. This should take about 10 minutes.

Ladle into serving bowls, garnish with spring onion, coriander and chilli oil, if desired, and serve immediately.

Karnataka in India's southwest is home to this vegetarian dish.
Made with a unique blend of dry-roasted spices, the rice, lentils
and vegetables take on tamarind's tang and ghee's richness.

RECIPE BY BILLY LAW

SERVES 6

200 g (1 cup) basmati
rice

160 g (¾ cup) toor dal
(pigeon peas)

½ tsp ground turmeric

2 tsp neutral oil

½ red onion, diced

1 carrot, diced

1 potato, peeled
and diced

40 g (¼ cup) frozen
green peas

½ tomato, diced

5–6 green beans,
chopped into 2–3 cm
(¾–1¼ in) pieces

1 tbsp tamarind paste

1 tsp brown sugar

3 tbsp Bisi bele bath
masala (page 145)

2 tsp salt

1 tbsp ghee

10 raw cashews, halved

3 dried Kashmiri
red chillies

1 tsp mustard seeds

1 sprig curry leaves

papadums, to serve

raita, to serve

Place the dal in a bowl and add enough water to cover
the dal by at least 2.5 cm (1 in). Soak for 20 minutes, then
drain and set aside.

Wash the rice until the water runs clear, then transfer to
a rice cooker. Add a pinch of salt and cook according to the
manufacturer's instructions.

Add the dal, turmeric and 750 ml (3 cups) of water to a
saucepan and bring to a simmer over medium heat. Reduce
the heat to low, cover and cook for about 15 minutes, stirring
occasionally, until the dal is soft and the liquid is absorbed.
If it gets too dry, add another 125 ml (½ cup) of water. Turn
off the heat and use the back of a wooden spoon to stir
and smear the dal on the side of the saucepan into a mash.
Cover and keep warm.

Meanwhile, heat the oil in a Dutch oven over medium–
high heat and add the onion, sauteing for about a minute
until translucent. Add the carrot, potato, peas, tomato and
beans and cook for about 2 minutes, until softened slightly.
Add 250 ml (1 cup) of water, reduce the heat to medium
and simmer for about 3 minutes, until the veggies are just
cooked through.

Mix the tamarind paste with 250 ml (1 cup) of water. Add
the brown sugar and masala, stirring until no lumps remain.
Pour into the Dutch oven, mix well and simmer for 2 minutes.

Add the rice and dal to the Dutch oven and mix well.
Add 500 ml (2 cups) of water and the salt and stir. Simmer
for 30 minutes over low heat until slightly thick yet pouring
consistency. If it gets too dry, add another 250 ml (1 cup)
of water, stir and continue cooking. Taste and adjust
seasoning accordingly.

Meanwhile, heat the ghee in a frying pan over medium
heat. Roast the cashews, chillies and mustard seeds for
about 2 minutes, until the cashews are golden brown. Add
the curry leaves and fry for 1 minute.

Meanwhile, cook the papadums according to the packet
instructions. Pour the cashew mixture onto the bisi bele bath
and serve immediately with the papadums and raita.

BISI BELE BATH

JOK

Thailand's rice porridge is prepared here with the most common additions: pork meatballs and a soft-boiled egg. However, the depth of flavour comes from the additional ingredients – pork stock, sesame oil and ginger, among others. This comforting dish is perfect to start the day or end the night with.

RECIPE BY SAREEN ROJANAMETIN & JEAN THAMTHANAKORN

SERVES 4

450 g (1 lb) jasmine rice

3 litres (3 qts) pork stock, plus extra if needed

4 eggs

freshly ground white pepper, to serve

1 tbsp sesame oil

2 spring onions (scallions), finely chopped

15 g (½ oz) young ginger, peeled and julienned

coriander (cilantro) leaves, to garnish

PORK MEATBALLS

5 garlic cloves, peeled

10 white peppercorns

400 g (14 oz) minced (ground) pork

2 tbsp soy sauce

1 tbsp caster (superfine) sugar

½ tsp baking soda

First, prepare the pork meatballs. Using a mortar and pestle, pound the garlic and white peppercorns into a fine paste. Add the minced pork and pound until homogenised, then add the remaining meatball ingredients and mix well. Cover and set aside in the refrigerator to marinate for a minimum of 3 hours.

Meanwhile, rinse the rice once or twice and drain to remove excess moisture. Using a blender or a mortar and pestle, process or pound the rice to a medium–fine consistency.

In a large stockpot or saucepan over high heat, combine the broken rice and stock and bring to the boil. Reduce the heat to low and simmer for about 20 minutes, stirring constantly to prevent the rice from sticking to the bottom of the pot, until the mixture becomes creamy. If the jok is too thick, add more pork stock or water as needed.

Take 1 tablespoon of the marinated pork mixture and roll it into a meatball using wet hands, repeating the process until all of the pork has been used. Add the meatballs to the jok and simmer for 10–15 minutes, until the meatballs are cooked through. Season with salt to taste.

Bring a saucepan half-filled with water to the boil over high heat. Remove from the heat and allow to cool for 1 minute. Place the eggs in the saucepan and leave uncovered for 12 minutes.

Using a slotted spoon, transfer the eggs to a bowl of cold or iced water to cool for a minimum of 5 minutes.

Divide the jok among four bowls and crack an egg into each one. Garnish with white pepper and the sesame oil, spring onion, ginger and coriander leaves, to taste.

VEGETABLE BIRYANI

In this biryani, vegetables are cooked until tender, infused with aromatics, and decorated with toasted cashews and raisins.

RECIPE BY JANE O'SHANNESSY

SERVES 4–6

300 g (1½ cups) basmati rice

80 ml (⅓ cup) neutral oil

5 cardamom pods

1 black cardamom pod (optional)

1 cinnamon stick

5 cloves

10 curry leaves

1 onion, finely sliced

1 long green chilli, finely sliced

4 garlic cloves, crushed

3 cm (1¼ in) piece ginger, finely grated

½ tsp chilli powder

2 tsp ground coriander

1 tsp ground fennel seeds

1 tsp cumin seeds

½ tsp ground turmeric

2 tomatoes, finely chopped

2 carrots, cut into batons

125 g (4½ oz) cauliflower florets

pinch of saffron threads

200 ml (7 fl oz) coconut milk

125 g (4½ oz) green beans, trimmed and halved

TO SERVE

papadums

chopped coriander (cilantro) leaves

80 g (½ cup) roasted cashews

2 tbsp raisins

mint leaves

garam masala (optional)

lemon wedges

Wash the rice until the water runs clear, then soak in a bowl of water for 30 minutes. Drain and set aside.

Heat the oil in a large heavy-based saucepan over medium–high heat. Bruise the cardamom pods, then add them to the oil along with the cinnamon, cloves and curry leaves. Cook for 1–2 minutes, until the spices start to crackle. Add the onion, then reduce the heat to low and cook for 10 minutes, until soft and slightly golden. Add the chilli, garlic and ginger and cook, stirring, for 2 minutes. Stir in the chilli powder, ground coriander, fennel seeds, cumin seeds and turmeric, and cook for 1 minute, then add the tomato and cook, stirring, for 5 minutes. Add the rice and stir to coat in the spices, then add the carrot and cauliflower.

In a small bowl, combine the saffron and coconut milk, then add to the pan, along with enough water to just cover the rice, carrot and cauliflower, about 350 ml (12 fl oz). Cover and simmer for 15–20 minutes, until the rice has absorbed the liquid. Add the beans, turn off the heat and stand, covered, for a further 5–8 minutes, until the beans are tender and the rice is cooked through. Season with salt to taste.

Meanwhile, cook the papadums according to the packet instructions.

Transfer the biryani to a serving platter and scatter over the coriander, cashews, raisins and mint leaves. Sprinkle with garam masala, if desired, and serve with lemon wedges for squeezing over and papadums on the side.

In Mumbai, street vendors prepare batches of this dish on large tawas, or flat pans. The result is a spicy mix of rice and vegetables, flavoured with pav bhaji masala – the blend of spices that packs Tawa pulao with flavour. Raita is a popular accompaniment, the yoghurt balancing out the dish's heat.

RECIPE BY BILLY LAW

SERVES 2–3

30 g (1 oz) butter

1 tbsp neutral oil

1 tsp cumin seeds

1 onion, finely chopped

3 garlic cloves, finely chopped

1 tsp grated ginger

50 g (⅓ cup) diced green bell pepper (capsicum)

1 tomato, diced

1½ tbsp pav bhaji masala

½ tsp ground Kashmiri chilli

40 g (¼ cup) frozen green peas, thawed

1 small carrot, shredded

1 potato, peeled, boiled and diced

1 tsp salt

½ tsp garam masala

15 g (¼ cup) coriander (cilantro) leaves, finely chopped

1 tbsp lemon juice

raita, to serve (optional)

TURMERIC RICE

200 g (1 cup) basmati rice

1 tsp salt

¼ tsp ground turmeric

To make the turmeric rice, wash the rice until the water runs clear, then soak in a bowl of water for 20 minutes. Drain and set aside.

Fill a large saucepan with 1 litre (1 qt) of water and bring to the boil over medium heat. Add the salt and turmeric and stir to mix well. Add the rice and cook, stirring occasionally, for 10–12 minutes, until all the liquid is absorbed and the rice is soft. Strain the rice and transfer to a large sieve. Fluff the rice and spread it out to allow the steam to escape. Set aside to cool to room temperature.

Melt the butter and heat the oil in a tawa or a large frying pan over medium–high heat. Add the cumin seeds and fry for 10 seconds. Add the onion and saute for about 30 seconds until translucent. Add the garlic and ginger and cook for another 30 seconds.

Add the bell pepper, tomato, pav bhaji masala, Kashmiri chilli and cook, stirring frequently, for about 3 minutes until the tomato is mushy and the oil is separated from the spice paste. Add the peas, carrot and potato, mix well and cook for another minute. If the mixture is too dry, add 2 tablespoons of hot water.

Reduce the heat to medium and add the turmeric rice, salt and garam masala. Mix well and cook for a minute, then drizzle the lemon juice and sprinkle half of the coriander over the rice. Mix well and transfer to a plate.

Garnish with the remaining coriander leaves and serve with raita, if desired, on the side.

NIGIRI

Nigiri's simplicity is deceiving. The list of ingredients is short, but each needs to be carefully prepared. While sushi can take years to master, this recipe has two great options to practise with, though the fish can be easily substituted with other varieties, or tamago for vegetarians.

RECIPE BY BILLY LAW

MAKES AROUND 16 PIECES

150 g (5½ oz) sashimi-grade salmon or 150 g (5½ oz) sashimi-grade tuna, or 75 g (2¾ oz) of each

370 g (2 cups) prepared sushi rice (page 103), at room temperature

dash of rice vinegar

wasabi, to taste

pickled ginger, to serve (optional)

soy sauce, for dipping (optional)

To prepare the salmon and/or tuna, cut the fish into a long fillet/s, about 7.5 cm (3 in) wide with the grain. Holding the knife at a 30- to 45-degree angle, slice the fillet/s in one stroke against the grain into 5–6 mm slices.

Set up your shaping station – place the fish slices on a plate and prepare two bowls, one with the sushi rice and one with water and a dash of rice vinegar. Set up a small plate of wasabi.

Dip your shaping hand in the vinegar water. With your dry hand, take 1 heaped tablespoon of sushi rice and press it into your shaping hand, rolling it in your palm into an oval-shaped rice ball.

Set the rice ball to the side and take a tuna or salmon slice. Place it in the palm of one hand and dot with a little wasabi in the centre. Place the rice ball on top, press down firmly with the index and middle fingers from the other hand. Turn the sushi over and continue shaping it into a neat oblong shape. Place the nigiri on a serving plate fish-side up and continue with the rest of the fish slices.

Serve the nigiri, if desired, with soy sauce and pickled ginger.

KIRIBATH

In Sri Lanka, Kiribath is a popular breakfast food. However, it also symbolises prosperity and luck, so it is eaten on the Sinhalese New Year and other days that mark beginnings, such as the start of the school year. Traditionally cut into diamonds, the creamy rice is served with a variety of accompaniments, including banana, jaggery and lunu miris. Here, a pol sambol provides a spicy, tangy contrast.

RECIPE BY BILLY LAW

SERVES 4

400 g (2 cups) jasmine rice

400 ml (13½ fl oz) coconut milk

2 pandan leaves, knotted (optional)

1 tsp salt

POL SAMBOL

6–8 dried red chillies

pinch of salt, to taste

1 tsp granulated sugar

250 g (9 oz) fresh shredded coconut, water squeezed out

5 Asian shallots, finely chopped

juice of 1 lime

Wash the rice until the water runs clear, then transfer to a large saucepan. Pour in 500 ml (2 cups) of water and half of the coconut milk and mix well. Add the pandan leaves and cook the rice over medium heat until most of the liquid is absorbed, stirring frequently to avoid rice sticking to the pan. Reduce the heat to medium–low and pour in the remaining coconut milk. Continue stirring and cook the rice until creamy and mushy, then season with the salt, cover and turn off the heat. Let rest for 10 minutes until all the moisture has evaporated, then uncover and leave to cool for 5 minutes.

Meanwhile, make the sambol. Grind the chillies, salt and sugar using a mortar and pestle until most of the chilli seeds are crushed. Add the coconut and stir to combine. Add the shallot and pound the paste for about 2 minutes until homogenous. Add the lime juice, mix well and adjust the seasoning to taste. Set aside.

Line a large shallow bowl with plastic wrap. Remove the pandan leaves from the rice and discard the leaves. Spoon the cooled rice into the bowl, pressing it down firmly. Place a large platter upside down over the bowl, then flip the rice onto the platter and remove the plastic wrap. Smooth out the rice with the back of a spoon and cut into diamond-shaped pieces.

Serve the kiribath with the sambol.

Named for Inari, the Shinto god who protects rice, Inari sushi are made of fried tofu pockets stuffed with rice. The tofu is flavoured with sweet soy sauce, providing a delicious complement to the sushi rice wrapped inside.

RECIPE BY BILLY LAW

MAKES 24

24 aburaage (deep-fried tofu pockets)

1 tbsp toasted white sesame seeds

toasted black sesame seeds, to garnish (optional)

pickled ginger, to serve (optional)

SUSHI RICE

440 g (2 cups) Japanese short-grain rice

1 × 5 cm × 5 cm (2 in × 2 in) piece kombu (dried kelp)

SUSHI VINEGAR

60 ml (¼ cup) rice wine vinegar

2 tbsp granulated sugar

1 tsp salt

Wash the rice until the water runs clear, then transfer to a rice cooker and add the kombu and 430 ml (14½ fl oz) of water. Cook according to the manufacturer's instructions.

Meanwhile, make the sushi vinegar. Heat the vinegar, sugar and salt in a small saucepan over medium heat. Stir until the sugar dissolves, turn off the heat and set aside.

If using a hangiri (wooden tub), moisten the tub with running water, then wipe off the excess water with a cloth. Alternatively, use a large baking tray.

Once the rice is cooked, remove the kombu and spread the hot rice in the hangiri. Gradually drizzle with the sushi vinegar, then use a rice paddle in a cutting motion to gently mix the sushi vinegar evenly into the rice. At the same time, fan the rice to cool it down and remove excess moisture. When the rice is no longer steaming hot, cover with a damp tea towel and set aside to cool to room temperature.

Once the rice is cool, sprinkle with the white sesame seeds. Gently slice and fold the rice to combine.

Fill a small bowl with water. Dip your shaping hand into the water. With your dry hand, scoop 2 tablespoons of the sushi rice and press into your shaping hand. Place your index and middle fingers from your dry hand on top of the rice and gently mould the rice into a short log, about 6 cm (2½ in) long. Place the rice log on a plate and repeat with the remaining rice.

Take a rice log and carefully stuff it into a tofu pocket. Seal the pocket like wrapping a present by folding in the corners and then folding lengthways to wrap the rice inside, then place the inari seam-side down on a plate. Repeat with the remaining tofu.

If desired, sprinkle some black sesame seeds on top of each inari and serve with pickled ginger on the side.

INARIZUSHI

Coated in rice and steamed, these meatballs arrive on the table looking like pearls glistening on the plate. While this dish commonly makes an appearance at Chinese New Year, it's simple enough to make any day of the year, though the rice does need time to soak.

RECIPE BY BILLY LAW

MAKES ABOUT 8

200 g (1 cup) glutinous rice

coriander (cilantro) leaves, to garnish (optional)

soy sauce, for dipping

sriracha chilli sauce, for dipping

PORK MEATBALLS

500 g (1 lb 2 oz) minced (ground) pork with 20% fat content

70 g (2½ oz) tinned water chestnuts, finely chopped

3 spring onions (scallions), white part only, finely chopped

2 tsp finely chopped ginger

2 tbsp Shaoxing rice wine

2 tsp cornflour (corn starch)

½ tsp ground white pepper

½ tbsp sesame oil

1 tsp salt

1 tbsp soy sauce

Wash the rice until the water runs clear, then place in a bowl and add enough water to cover the rice by at least 2.5 cm (1 in). Soak for at least 2 hours, but no more than 6 hours.

To make the meatballs, add all the ingredients to a large mixing bowl. Using chopsticks or a wooden spatula, stir vigorously in one direction for about 3 minutes, until the mixture becomes sticky. Cover and marinate in the fridge for 30 minutes.

Drain the rice, shaking off any excess water and spread out on a tray.

Roll the pork mixture into golf ball-sized meatballs, then roll the meatballs in the rice until evenly coated.

To prepare the steamer, cut out a circle of baking paper the same size as the mouth of the steamer. Punch a few holes with a hole puncher, then line the bottom of the steamer with the paper. Place the meatballs in the steamer and cover.

Starting with cold water, steam the meatballs over medium heat for 20 minutes. Turn off the heat and let sit without opening the lid for another 3 minutes.

To serve, garnish with coriander, if desired, and serve with soy sauce and sriracha.

MAKIZUSHI

Makizushi, also known as norimaki, are sushi rolls. This recipe features fillings traditional to hosomaki – thin rolls with just one filling – but two to three ingredients of your choice can be added to make chumaki, which are slightly fatter. Filling options include crabmeat, unagi (eel) and kanpyo (gourd strips), but the options are wide and easily tailored to personal preference.

RECIPE BY BILLY LAW

MAKES 32 PIECES

740 g (4 cups) prepared sushi rice (page 103)

4 nori sheets, cut in half

wasabi, to serve

soy sauce, to serve

FILLINGS OF YOUR CHOICE

sashimi-grade tuna, sliced lengthways into thin strips

sashimi-grade salmon, sliced lengthways into thin strips

oshinko (pickled daikon radish), sliced lengthways into sticks

cucumber, seeded and sliced lengthways into sticks

kanikama crab sticks, sliced into smaller strips

natto (see Note)

Wrap a sushi mat with plastic wrap to prevent the sushi rice from sticking when rolling. Prepare a bowl of water and set aside.

Lay a nori sheet (glossy-side down) on the mat. Dip your fingers into the bowl of water and use them to spread about 67 g (½ cup) of the sushi rice evenly over the nori, leaving about one-third of the nori bare at the top.

Add your filling of choice to the bottom half of the nori, avoiding overfilling.

Lift the edge of the sushi mat that is closest to you and roll the nori over the filling away from you. Apply firm pressure to the roll and use your fingers to tuck the filling in as you go.

Place the finished roll on a chopping board and cut in half. Cut in half two more times to make eight sushi pieces. Transfer the pieces to a serving plate and repeat with the remaining nori, rice and fillings.

Serve with wasabi and soy sauce on the side.

NOTE: Natto is fermented soybeans, a traditional dish in Japan. It can be found in Japanese supermarkets.

Breakfast or snack breaks in Indonesia often feature Arem-arem. With no strict guide when it comes to fillings, these cylindrical rice cakes are easy to adjust to personal preference, whether that's vegetables, beef floss or, as in this recipe, chicken. If you're unable to find banana leaves to steam the cakes in, baking paper also works.

RECIPE BY BILLY LAW

MAKES ABOUT 12

8 × 30 cm (12 in) banana leaves, cut into 20 cm × 20 cm (8 in × 8 in) sheets

COCONUT RICE

500 g (2½ cups) jasmine rice

700 ml (23½ fl oz) coconut milk

1 tsp salt

FILLING

3 garlic cloves

5 French shallots

1 lemongrass stalk, white part only

2 cm (¾ in) piece turmeric

2 cm (¾ in) piece galangal

2 tbsp neutral oil

250 g (9 oz) minced (ground) chicken

1 carrot, finely diced

1 tsp salt

1 tsp granulated sugar

pinch of ground white pepper

To make the coconut rice, add all the ingredients to a saucepan with 300 ml (10 fl oz) of water and bring to the boil over medium heat. Reduce the heat to low and cook, stirring occasionally, until all the liquid has been absorbed by the rice. Turn off the heat and set aside to cool to room temperature.

Meanwhile, make the filling. In a food processor, blend the garlic, shallots, lemongrass, turmeric, galangal and 1 tablespoon of water into a paste. Heat the oil in a frying pan over medium–high heat, add the spice paste and cook for about 1 minute until fragrant. Add the remaining filling ingredients and 1 tablespoon of water, and stir-fry for 2–3 minutes until the chicken is cooked and most of the liquid in the pan has evaporated. Turn off the heat and set the filling aside to cool to room temperature.

Set up a steamer over medium heat.

On a work surface, take a banana leaf and spread 1 heaped tablespoon of rice along the edge closest to you. Spread a layer of the filling on top and cover it with another layer of rice. Roll the leaf away from you as tightly as possible, then fold both edges and secure the ends with toothpicks. Repeat with the remaining rice and filling. Place the banana leaf parcels in the steamer basket and cover.

Steam the rolls for 1 hour. Remove from the heat and let cool before serving.

ONIGIRI

Japan's perfectly portable triangles of rice wrapped in nori: Onigiri. They make for a great snack or light meal and are ideal for picnics or work and school lunches. This recipe includes two types of filling – spicy tuna and furikake – but onigiri are delicious with just a sprinkle of salt, or nothing added at all.

RECIPE BY BILLY LAW

MAKES 12

600 g (1 lb 5 oz) prepared sushi rice (page 103)

1 nori sheet, cut into 12 × 4 cm × 12 cm (1½ in × 4¾ in) strips

SPICY TUNA MAYO ONIGIRI

95 g (3¼ oz) tinned tuna, drained and mashed

1 tbsp Kewpie mayonnaise, plus extra to serve

1 tbsp sriracha chilli sauce

shichimi togarashi, to garnish

FURIKAKE ONIGIRI

45 g (½ cup) furikake seasoning (any flavour)

1 tbsp sesame oil

To make the tuna onigiri, stir the tuna, mayo and sriracha in a bowl until well combined.

To make the furikake onigiri, place the rice, furikake and sesame oil in a bowl, stirring until well combined.

Drape a 20 cm × 20 cm (8 in × 8 in) sheet of plastic wrap in a small bowl. Place about 67 g (½ cup) of the sushi rice in the bowl; if making the furikake onigiri, use the seasoned rice.

If making the tuna onigiri, use a finger to make an indentation in the middle of the rice, then fill it with a spoonful of the tuna mayo.

Lift the corners of the plastic wrap, then twist a few times to seal the filling inside the rice ball. Using both hands, press firmly and shape the rice ball into a triangle.

Remove the plastic wrap and place the rice ball, flat-side down, in the middle of a nori strip. Wrap the nori around the rice and tuck both edges under.

If making tuna onigiri, squeeze a dollop of mayo on top of the rice, then sprinkle with shichimi togarashi.

Repeat with the remaining ingredients.

Served with an array of sides that include caramelised pork and mango, the heart of this Thai dish is rice fried with gapi. The shrimp paste packs the rice with umami, which sings with the sweet, sour and spicy flavours of the other ingredients.

RECIPE BY SAREEN ROJANAMETIN & JEAN THAMTHANAKORN

SERVES 2–3

2 lap cheong (Chinese sausages), cut into 5 mm (¼ in) slices

170 ml (⅔ cup) neutral oil

50 g (1¾ oz) dried shrimp, soaked in warm water for 15 minutes and drained

3 eggs, beaten

5 garlic cloves, finely chopped

1 tbsp gapi (fermented shrimp paste)

60 ml (¼ cup) pork stock or water

500 g (1 lb 2 oz) steamed jasmine rice, cooled

CARAMELISED PORK

80 ml (⅓ cup) neutral oil

12 small Asian shallots, finely sliced

400 g (14 oz) pork belly, cut into 1 cm (½ in) cubes

2 tbsp soy sauce

2 tbsp oyster sauce

2 tbsp dark soy sauce

200 g (7 oz) palm sugar, grated

TO SERVE

1 sour green mango, sliced

2 small Asian shallots, finely sliced

30 g (¼ cup) finely sliced snake (yard-long) beans

2–3 lime wedges

5 red and green bird's eye chillies, roughly chopped

To prepare the pork, heat the oil in a wok over medium heat and saute the shallots until fragrant. Add the pork and stir-fry for 6–7 minutes, then stir in the remaining ingredients. Add 125 ml (½ cup) of water, reduce the heat to medium–low and cook for 5–10 minutes, until the liquid evaporates and the mixture caramelises and is sticky. Set aside.

Bring a small saucepan of water to the boil over high heat and blanch the lap cheong for 2 minutes. Remove from the heat, drain and pat dry with paper towel. Heat 140 ml (4½ fl oz) of the oil in a clean wok over medium heat. Add the lap cheong and fry for 2–3 minutes, until golden. Remove from the oil with a slotted spoon and drain on paper towel. Using the left-over oil, fry the shrimp for 2–3 minutes, until golden brown. Remove from the oil with a slotted spoon and drain on paper towel. Reserve the oil for frying.

Add 1 tablespoon of the reserved oil to the wok and return to the heat. Tilt the wok so the oil coats the base and side, then add one-third of the egg and tilt the wok to create a thin omelette. Cook until set, then transfer to a plate. Repeat the process so that you have three omelettes. Stack on top of each other, cut into quarters and slice into strips. Set aside. Discard any remaining reserved oil.

In a clean wok, heat the remaining 30 ml (1 fl oz) of the fresh oil over medium heat and saute the garlic until golden and fragrant. Add the gapi, mashing it to remove any lumps, and fry for 2 minutes, until fragrant. Pour in the stock and stir until the gapi dissolves, then add the rice and reduce the heat to low. Stir thoroughly to evenly distribute the gapi throughout the rice. Once the rice has changed colour and is hot, remove from the heat.

To serve, pack a small soup bowl to the brim with the rice and cover with a serving plate. Flip the plate and the bowl, then remove the bowl so that you have a mound of rice in the middle of the plate. Arrange the omelette, shrimp, lap cheong, pork, mango, shallots, snake beans and lime around the rice. Sprinkle the rice with the chillies and serve.

Originally from Shanghai, these sticky rolls are a warm way to start the day. The fillings wrapped inside the rice vary, but this version's savoury Chinese doughnut, pork floss and pickled vegetables make for a tasty meal to enjoy for breakfast or whenever hunger strikes on the go.

RECIPE BY ARCHAN CHAN

SERVES 4

500 g (2½ cups) glutinous rice, soaked in cold water overnight

100 g (3½ oz) preserved or pickled vegetables

1 litre (1 qt) neutral oil

1 store-bought savoury Chinese doughnut

50 g (1¾ oz) pork floss

Pour water into a large saucepan to a depth of about 3 cm (1¼ in) and bring to the boil. Line a bamboo basket or a sieve with muslin (cheesecloth) – choose one that can sit inside the pan without touching the water.

Add the rice and spread it out evenly, then make a little hole in the middle (this will help the steam to come through and ensure the rice is cooked properly). Cover and steam for 25–30 minutes until the rice is tender.

If you are using a packet of ready-to-eat preserved vegetables, just give them a rough chop. If you are using whole preserved vegetables, you might need to give them a rinse or even a soak before chopping, depending on how salty they are.

Pour the oil into a medium saucepan and heat to 170°C (340°F), or until a cube of bread dropped in the oil browns in 20 seconds. Add the Chinese doughnut and fry for about 1 minute, turning constantly, to give it a crunchier texture. Remove with tongs and drain on paper towel. Alternatively, preheat the oven to 180°C (350°F) and heat the doughnut for 2 minutes.

Split the doughnut in half lengthways, then cut each piece in half, or into 12 cm (4¾ in) lengths.

Lay a sushi mat on a work surface, then a piece of plastic wrap (about 25 cm × 25 cm/10 in × 10 in). Spread one-quarter of the rice over the plastic wrap in a rectangle as if you were making a sushi roll.

Arrange the pork floss lengthways in the centre of the rectangle. Top with the preserved vegetables, then the doughnut. Using the sushi mat, roll up the rice to enclose the filling and make a firm roll. Hold and twist both ends of the plastic wrap in opposite directions to tighten the roll and press firmly to seal. Repeat with the remaining ingredients.

Rest for about 10 minutes. These rolls are traditionally eaten whole, so you can unwrap them as you eat, but you can also unwrap them to cut into pieces.

OMURAISU

While the Omuraisu splashed across the internet is a perfectly formed, wobbly omelette that slices open to perfectly jacket the rice it sits on, this theatricality is not a requisite. This recipe does not require hours of practice, staying true to the heart of the dish, which is an omelette served with fried rice.

RECIPE BY BILLY LAW

MAKES 1

1½ tbsp neutral oil

½ onion, finely chopped

1 boneless, skinless chicken thigh, tendons and fat removed, diced into 1 cm (½ in) pieces

50 g (1¾ oz) leg ham, diced (optional)

10 g (¼ oz) butter

90 g (½ cup) steamed short-grain rice

2 tbsp tomato ketchup, plus extra to serve

3 large eggs

okonomi sauce (see Note; optional)

handful of parsley, finely chopped

Heat 1 tablespoon of the oil in a non-stick frying pan over medium–high heat. Add the onion and saute for about 30 seconds until fragrant and translucent. Add the chicken and stir-fry for 1 minute or until the chicken is half cooked. Add the leg ham, if using, and cook for another minute. Add the butter and stir until fully melted. Add the rice, stirring to separate the grains until well combined. Add the tomato ketchup, season with salt and pepper to taste and stir-fry for 2 minutes, or until most of the sauce has been absorbed by the rice. Transfer the rice mixture to a plate and, with your hands, shape the rice into an oval. Set aside and keep warm.

Using chopsticks, beat the eggs with a pinch of salt in a bowl for about 30 seconds until fluffy.

Wipe the pan clean and heat the remaining oil over low heat. Pour in the egg, swirling around to cover the full pan, and cook for a minute. Use a spatula to gently pry the edge of the omelette to dislodge it from the pan – you should be able to swirl the omelette around the pan. When the surface is almost cooked through but still slightly wet, in one swift move, flip the omelette over and cook the other side.

Add the rice to the centre of the omelette. Fold both sides of the omelette to cover the rice – it should be the shape of an eye. Now flip the omelette over with the folded side down and carefully transfer to a serving plate.

Drizzle with okonomi sauce, if desired, sprinkle with the parsley and serve with ketchup on the side, if desired.

NOTE: Okonomi sauce is a sweet and savoury Japanese condiment most often served with okonomiyaki (savoury pancakes). It can be found in Asian supermarkets.

Lotus leaves unfold to reveal Lo mai gai, the fragrant dim sum classic, which combines glutinous rice and marinated meat.

RECIPE BY ARCHAN CHAN

MAKES 4

2 dried shiitake mushrooms

400 g (2 cups) glutinous rice, soaked in cold water overnight

1 tsp lard

½ tsp fine sea salt

50 g (1¾ oz) bamboo shoots, finely diced

150 g (5½ oz) boneless, skinless chicken thighs, sliced

100 g (3½ oz) pork collar butt (preferably with about 30% fat content), sliced

3 tbsp neutral oil

1 tsp crushed garlic

2 thin slices ginger

1 tsp Shaoxing rice wine

4 dried lotus leaves

2 salted duck egg yolks

MARINADE

¼ tsp fine sea salt

½ tsp caster (superfine) sugar

½ tsp soy sauce

⅛ tsp ground white pepper

¼ tsp Shaoxing rice wine

⅛ tsp cornflour (corn starch)

SAUCE

1 tbsp oyster sauce

1 tsp soy sauce

¼ tsp caster sugar

⅛ tsp ground white pepper

⅛ tsp sesame oil

1 tsp cornflour

Soak the dried shiitake in 250 ml (1 cup) of tepid water for 6 hours or overnight. Drain, then finely dice.

Drain the rice and mix in the lard and salt in a bowl.

Pour water into a large saucepan to a depth of about 3 cm (1¼ in) and bring to the boil. Place the rice on a steamer tray or plate, cover and steam for 30 minutes or until tender.

Meanwhile, bring another saucepan of water to the boil, and blanch the shiitake and bamboo shoots for 30 seconds. Drain and refresh under cold running water.

Combine all the marinade ingredients. Add the chicken and pork and turn to coat well. Set aside for 30 minutes.

Heat 1 tablespoon of the oil in a large frying pan over high heat, add the chicken and pork and cook for 2 minutes or until browned. Remove from the pan and set aside.

Combine all the sauce ingredients and 80 ml (⅓ cup) of water in a bowl. Add to the pan and cook, stirring, over medium–high heat for 30 seconds or until the sauce has thickened. Set aside to cool.

Wipe out the pan and add the remaining oil and place over medium heat. Add the garlic and ginger and saute for 10 seconds or until fragrant. Add the shiitake and bamboo shoots and saute for 30 seconds. Deglaze the pan with the Shaoxing wine. Return the chicken and pork to the pan and cook for another 30 seconds, then add the sauce and cook for a further 30 seconds.

Blanch the lotus leaves in boiling water for 10 seconds, then rinse under cold running water and pat dry. Cut each in half, ensuring the leaves are completely dry.

Halve the yolks. Place two leaf halves on top of each other. Put a thin layer of rice in the centre of the stacked leaves, then top with a quarter of the chicken and pork mixture and a piece of yolk. Cover with another layer of rice, then fold in the sides of the leaf and wrap to enclose the filling. Repeat with the remaining leaves and filling.

Pour water into a large saucepan to a depth of about 3 cm (1¼ in) and bring to the boil. Arrange the lotus leaf parcels on a steamer tray or plate (without overlapping), then cover and steam for 15 minutes. Unwrap the lotus leaf to eat.

Korea's Gimbap, like Japan's Makizushi (page 106), combines nori, rice and fillings to great effect. Easily transportable, it makes a great option for picnics and meals on the go. The fillings vary, but the classics include a colourful mix of meat and vegetables.

RECIPE BY BILLY LAW

SERVES 6–8

60 ml (¼ cup) rice vinegar

1 tbsp caster (superfine) sugar

370 g (2 cups) steamed short-grain rice

1 Lebanese (short) cucumber

1 bunch English spinach, roots trimmed

2 tsp sesame oil

2 eggs

1 tsp neutral oil

5 nori sheets

5 strips of pre-cut danmuji (yellow pickled radish) (see Note)

5 strips of pre-cut barbecued gimbap ham (see Note)

5 strips of pre-cut seasoned burdock root (see Note)

mayonnaise, to serve

soy sauce, to serve

wasabi, to serve

NOTE: If your radish comes as a big chunk, cut into 5 mm (¼ in) thick strips.

You can substitute gimbap ham with smoked ham or SPAM.

All these ingredient will be available in Korean supermarkets.

Combine the rice vinegar, sugar and a pinch of salt in a small saucepan and stir over low heat until the sugar dissolves. Set aside.

While the rice is still warm, spread it out on a tray, sprinkle with the rice vinegar mixture and leave to cool to room temperature.

Cut the cucumber in half lengthways and scrap out the seeds with a spoon. Cut the halves into 5 mm (¼ in) thick strips and set aside.

Bring a saucepan of water to the boil over medium–high heat. Blanch the spinach for 1 minute. Drain and refresh under cold running water, then squeeze out as much water as possible. Place the spinach in a bowl, season with the sesame oil and a pinch of salt, and mix well. Set aside.

Beat the eggs and a pinch of salt in a small bowl. Heat the oil in a non-stick frying pan over medium–low heat and fry the egg for 2–3 minutes. Once the bottom has set, flip and cook for 1 further minute. Transfer to a chopping board and slice into 1 cm (½ in) thick strips.

To assemble, place a nori sheet, shiny-side down and with the longer side facing you, on a sushi mat. Spread about 185 g (1 cup) of the rice evenly over the nori, leaving a 4 cm (1½ in) edge at the top of the nori.

Place one or two strips each of the cucumber, egg, danmuji, ham and burdock root along the edge closest to you, and top with a few spinach leaves. Be careful not to overfill your gimbap.

Lift the edge of the sushi mat closest to you and roll the nori over the filling away from you. Apply firm pressure and use your fingers to tuck the filling in as you go. Brush the top edge of the nori with a little water, then finish rolling to seal the gimbap tightly. Repeat to make five rolls.

Cut each roll into 2 cm (¾ in) thick pieces and serve with mayonnaise, soy sauce or wasabi on the side.

PULUT TAI TAI

Although they don't add flavour, butterfly pea flowers imbue this Malaysian dessert with a beautiful blue colour. The rice cakes are delicious thanks to the fragrant milk the rice is cooked in and the kaya – a caramel coconut jam, which is served with the sweet squares.

RECIPE BY AIM ARIS & AHMAD SALIM

SERVES 4

1 tbsp dried butterfly pea flowers or 1½ tsp butterfly pea powder

500 g (2½ cups) glutinous rice

1 tsp tamarind paste

1 pandan leaf, knotted and torn

banana leaves, for lining

310 ml (1¼ cups) coconut milk

¾ tsp salt

neutral oil, for brushing

Hainanese Kaya (page 144), to serve

In a kettle or saucepan, bring 250 ml (1 cup) of water to the boil. Place the butterfly pea flowers or powder in a heatproof bowl, add the boiling water and leave to brew for 5 minutes. Strain, reserving the liquid.

Wash the rice until the water runs clear, then drain. Divide the rice and tamarind paste evenly between two bowls. Pour the butterfly pea flower liquid into one bowl, along with enough water to cover the rice, and stir to combine. In the second bowl, add just enough water to cover the rice. Leave to soak for 6–8 hours.

Set up a steamer over medium–high heat. Add the pandan leaf to the steaming water and bring to the boil. Line your steamer basket with banana leaves (or baking paper) and poke holes in them.

Meanwhile, drain both bowls of soaked rice and mix them together. Place the rice in the steamer basket and steam for 10 minutes.

While the rice is cooking, mix the coconut milk and salt in a small bowl. When the rice is done, tip the rice into a bowl and pour over half of the coconut milk. Stir well, then return the rice to the basket and steam for another 10 minutes. Repeat the process with the remaining coconut milk and steam for another 10 minutes. By now, the rice should be soft but chewy in texture with an attractive blue and white marbling effect.

Line a 20.5 cm (8 in) square cake tin with foil, leaving an overhang at the sides. Lightly brush the lined tin with oil. Add the steamed rice and spread it out evenly. Top with a slightly smaller cake tin (about 17.5 cm/7 in), then place a heavy object (such as a mortar) in the tin. Leave it to press down on the rice for 2–3 hours.

Remove the pulut tai tai from the tin, cut into cubes and serve with kaya.

SUA CHUA NEP CAM

With a name that translates to Yoghurt with black sticky rice, this Vietnamese dessert offers both taste and texture. The sweet, chewy rice and the tart, silky yoghurt make for a harmonious combination. While delicious as is, feel free to serve the rice with fruit of your choice.

RECIPE BY JERRY MAI

SERVES 4

350 g (12½ oz) glutinous black rice, soaked in cold water overnight

2 pandan leaves

60 g (2 oz) palm sugar, grated

pinch of salt

fruit of your choice, to serve (optional)

VIETNAMESE YOGHURT

395 g (14 oz) tin condensed milk

60 g (¼ cup) natural yoghurt

To make the yoghurt, pour the condensed milk into a large bowl. Fill the condensed milk tin with hot water and add to the condensed milk. Add another tin of hot water followed by a tin of room temperature water. Whisk until well combined, then whisk in the yoghurt. Strain the mixture into a large glass jar. Seal.

Place the jar in a large saucepan and pour enough boiling water into the pan to come three-quarters of the way up the side of the jar. Cover and set aside for 8 hours or, preferably, overnight.

Remove the jar from the pan and set aside in the fridge until set and completely chilled.

Meanwhile, drain and rinse the rice, then place in a large saucepan with the pandan leaves and 1 litre (1 qt) of water. Set over medium–high heat and bring to the boil. Reduce the heat to a simmer and cook for 30 minutes, then stir through the palm sugar and salt and cook for a further 20 minutes, or until the rice is soft with a gentle bite and the water is absorbed. Transfer the rice to a bowl and set aside in the fridge until cool.

To serve, spoon the sticky rice into tall glasses and top with the Vietnamese yoghurt and fruit, if desired, to serve.

Among porridges, the Filipino Champorado stands out thanks to its signature ingredient: chocolate. As this breakfast dish uses unsweetened cocoa, the end result is not oversweet, but rather creamy and a touch bitter. Evaporated milk can be poured over at the end for a richer finish.

RECIPE BY BILLY LAW

SERVES 8–10

200 g (1 cup) glutinous rice

40 g (⅓ cup) Dutch (unsweetened) cocoa powder

165 g (¾ cup) granulated sugar

pinch of salt

185 ml (¾ cup) coconut milk, plus extra to serve

condensed milk, to serve (optional)

Wash the rice until the water runs clear. Drain and set aside.

In a saucepan, bring 1 litre (1 qt) of water to the boil over medium–high heat. Add the cocoa powder and stir constantly until the cocoa dissolves and no lumps remain.

Add the rice and stir to combine. Reduce the heat to medium–low and cook for 13–15 minutes until the all the water is absorbed, stirring frequently to avoid the rice sticking to the pan.

Add the sugar, salt and coconut milk and stir for about 2 minutes, until the sugar dissolves.

Transfer ladles of the chocolate porridge to serving bowls and top with coconut milk or condensed milk for extra decadence.

NOTE: Champorado is commonly served with candied, salted anchovies on the side for that sweet and salty combo that you find in many Asian desserts.

KHAO NIAOW MA MUANG

Cold slices of mango on a bed of warm sticky rice with coconut-sugar syrup drizzled over: Mango and sticky rice is famous beyond Thailand's borders for good reason. More than the sum of its parts, this dish balances the richness of coconut milk with the freshness of the mango.

RECIPE BY BILLY LAW

SERVES 4

2 large mangoes
(see Note)

toasted white sesame
seeds, to garnish
(optional)

STICKY RICE

200 g (1 cup) glutinous
rice

125 ml (½ cup) coconut
milk

2 tbsp granulated sugar

½ tsp salt

SWEET COCONUT
CREAM

125 ml (½ cup) coconut
milk

2 tbsp granulated sugar

pinch of salt, to taste

Wash the rice until the water runs clear, then transfer to a bowl and add enough water to cover the rice by at least 2.5 cm (1 in). Soak for at least 6 hours.

Lined a steamer basket with muslin (cheesecloth) to prevent sticking and set up the steamer over medium heat.

Drain the rice and transfer to the steamer basket. Cover and steam the rice for 20–30 minutes until done. Remove from the heat and set aside to cool to room temperature.

Meanwhile, make the sweet coconut cream. Add all the ingredients to a small saucepan and stir over medium heat. Once the mixture starts to boil, pour into a bowl and set aside to cool to room temperature.

Peel the mangoes and cut lengthways – you should have two large pieces of flesh from each mango. Keeping each portion separate, cut into bite-sized pieces.

Place a serving of sticky rice on each plate and top with a portion of mango. Sprinkle over some sesame seeds, if desired, and serve with the coconut cream.

NOTE: It's best to use mango that is just ripe and still slightly firm. The most common variety in Thailand (Nam Dok Mai) is sweet and slightly sour.

KHEER

Throughout India, Kheer is served in celebratory spreads and at the end of everyday meals. The simplest versions feature only three ingredients: milk, sugar and rice, cooked until the milk reduces to a thick and creamy texture. However, spices and other additions like rose water are common, added alongside nuts which stud the surface of this fragrant dessert.

RECIPE BY BILLY LAW

SERVES 6

100 g (½ cup) basmati rice

1 litre (1 qt) full-cream (whole) milk, plus extra if needed

3 cardamom pods

10 saffron threads

90 g (3 oz) granulated sugar

10 raw cashews, halved

10 pistachio kernels, chopped, plus extra to garnish

2 tbsp raisins

Wash the rice until the water runs clear. Drain and set aside.

Bring the milk, cardamom pods and saffron to a gentle simmer in a large saucepan over medium–low heat. Add the rice, stirring occasionally, and cook for about 20 minutes until the rice is soft. Discard the cardamom.

Add the sugar, cashews, pistachios and raisins, stirring until the sugar dissolves. Reduce the heat to low and cook for another 5 minutes, continuing to stir. If the kheer becomes too thick, add a splash of milk and stir until it reaches your preferred consistency.

Divide the kheer between serving bowls, garnish with pistachios and serve warm.

Nang let are ubiquitous in Thailand, where street vendors sell these simple but delicious rice cakes drizzled in sugar syrup. While easy to make, they do take time: after cooking, the rice needs to dry out completely. This can take the better part of a day, but the hands-on time is short, and the results are delicious.

RECIPE BY BILLY LAW

MAKES ABOUT 10

300 g (1½ cups) glutinous rice

½ tsp salt

neutral oil, for frying

200 g (7 oz) palm sugar, shaved

1 tbsp dark brown sugar

2 tbsp toasted white and black sesame seeds, to garnish

Cook the rice according to the instructions on page 130.

In a bowl, mix the cooked rice and salt, then spread into a thin layer (1 cm/¼ in thick) on a tray lined with baking paper. Cool to room temperature.

Dip a circular cookie cutter (see Note) about 7 cm (2¾ in) in diameter in a bowl of water and cut the sticky rice into rounds, dipping the cutter in the water each time. Place the rice cakes on another tray lined with baking paper and sun-dry the cakes until they are completely free of moisture; this will take at least 6 hours or multiple days, depending on the weather. Alternatively, use a dehydrator or an oven set to 50°C (122°F) for at least 8 hours.

Once the cakes are dry, fill a wok or deep frying pan with at least 1¼ cm (3 in) of oil and bring to 180°C (350°F) over medium heat; a cube of bread dropped in the oil will brown in 15 seconds. In batches, carefully lower the dry rice cakes into the hot oil. Flip the cakes frequently for 1–2 minutes until all the rice is puffed up, lightly golden and crispy. Transfer the rice cakes to a wire rack lined with paper towels to absorb any excess oil and let cool completely.

Heat the palm sugar and brown sugar with 2 tablespoons of water in a saucepan over medium heat, stirring until the sugar melts. Cook the mixture, stirring occasionally, for about 10 minutes until caramelised and golden brown.

Let the sugar syrup cool slightly, then drizzle it over the rice cakes and sprinkle with sesame seeds.

NOTE: If you don't have a cookie cutter, the ring of a mason jar is a great alternative.

ZARDA

This festive dessert is popular in northern India, where bowls of the bright yellow rice are enjoyed during celebrations such as Eid. Sweetened with sugar, rich with melted ghee and aromatic with cloves, cardamom and saffron, this dessert is quick to prepare.

RECIPE BY BILLY LAW

SERVES 4

200 g (1 cup) basmati rice

2 cardamom pods

4 cloves

10 saffron threads

2 drops orange food colouring (optional)

3 tbsp ghee

10 raw cashews, halved

1 tbsp slivered almonds

15 g (¼ cup) shredded coconut

2 tsp raisins

220 g (1 cup) granulated sugar

chopped toasted almonds, to garnish

Wash the rice until the water runs clear, then soak in a bowl of water for at least 30 minutes.

Drain the rice and transfer to a large frying pan. Add the cardamom pods, cloves, saffron, food colouring, if using, and 375 ml (1½ cups) of water and bring to the boil over medium–high heat. Reduce the heat to low, cover and cook for 8–10 minutes, stirring occasionally, until all the liquid is absorbed. Fluff the rice and discard the cardamom pods and cloves.

Meanwhile, in another pan, heat the ghee over medium–low heat. Add the cashews, slivered almonds, coconut, raisins and sugar and toast the mixture for about 3 minutes until fragrant and golden. Drain through a fine-mesh sieve and add the nut and sugar mixture to the rice, stirring to combine.

Reduce the heat to low. Gently stir the rice, then cover and cook for 2 minutes. Repeat 2–3 times, until the rice is fully cooked. Remove from the heat and let rest for 10 minutes. Garnish the zarda with toasted almonds and serve.

BIKO

Glutinous rice forms the base of this Filipino dessert, sweetened with coconut milk and brown sugar. Served hot and gooey, Biko is topped with caramel and finished with latik, which is made by cooking coconut milk curds until they're golden and toasted – the perfect complement to the chewy rice cake.

RECIPE BY BILLY LAW

MAKE 12 SQUARES

400 g (2 cups) glutinous rice

125 ml (½ cup) coconut milk

½ tsp salt

2 pandan leaves, knotted

250 ml (1 cup) fresh coconut milk (see Note)

neutral oil, for greasing

COCONUT SYRUP

500 ml (2 cups) coconut milk

185 g (1 cup, lightly packed) dark brown sugar

110 g (½ cup) granulated sugar

Wash the rice until the water runs clear, then transfer to a bowl and add enough water to cover the rice by at least 2.5 cm (1 in). Soak for a minimum of 6 hours, then drain and set aside.

Add the rice, coconut milk, salt, pandan leaves and 125 ml (½ cup) of water to a large saucepan and bring to a simmer over medium heat. Reduce the heat to low, cover and cook for about 10 minutes, stirring occasionally to avoid the rice sticking to the bottom of the pan, until the liquid is absorbed by the rice. Once the rice is par-cooked, discard the pandan leaves, cover and keep warm.

To make the latik, heat the fresh coconut milk in a large saucepan over medium–low heat for about 5 minutes, stirring occasionally until the milk is separated. Keep stirring for about 3 minutes until the curds are dark brown and smell like toasted coconut. Strain the curds through a fine-mesh sieve and dry on paper towel to remove excess oil. Set aside.

To make the coconut syrup, cook the coconut milk and sugars in a large frying pan over medium heat for about 10 minutes, stirring continuously until the liquid thickens into a dark brown caramel syrup. Turn off the heat and reserve 125 ml (½ cup) of the syrup. Add the sticky rice to the pan, gently stir and fold the rice into the syrup until evenly coated.

Preheat the oven to 180°C (350°F). Grease a 20 cm (8 in) square baking tin with oil. Using the back of a wooden spatula, spread the rice evenly and firmly press into the tin. Drizzle over the reserved syrup and spread evenly over the rice.

Bake for 25–30 minutes until the topping is caramelised and bubbling. Remove from the oven and set aside to cool for an hour before cutting into squares. Top each square with a sprinkle of crispy latik and serve.

NOTE: If using tinned coconut milk, it needs to contain no additives.

BIBIM SAUCE

MAKES APPROX. 200 ML (7 FL OZ)

135 g (½ cup) gochujang (Korean chilli paste)

2 tbsp sesame oil

1 tbsp caster (superfine) sugar

1 tsp white vinegar

1 garlic clove, finely chopped

Combine all the ingredients in a small bowl and stir until the sugar dissolves.

The bibim sauce will keep in an airtight container in the fridge for up to 2 weeks.

SPRING ONION OIL

MAKES 125 ML (½ CUP)

3 spring onions (scallions), finely sliced

pinch of salt

100 ml (3½ fl oz) vegetable oil

Place the spring onion and salt in a metal bowl.

Heat the oil in a small saucepan to 150°C (300°F); a cube of bread dropped in the oil will brown in 15 seconds. Pour the oil over the spring onion. Stir and set aside to infuse until you are ready to use.

The spring onion oil should be used the same day it is made.

NUOC MAM DIPPING SAUCE

MAKES 600 ML (20½ FL OZ)

2 garlic cloves, finely chopped

3 bird's eye chillies, finely chopped or sliced

150 ml (5 fl oz) fish sauce

100 ml (3½ fl oz) white vinegar

140 g (5 oz) caster (superfine) sugar

Combine the ingredients and 200 ml (7 fl oz) of water in a bowl and stir until the sugar dissolves.

The nuoc mam will keep in an airtight container in the fridge for up to 2 weeks.

SPICY SOY AND SPRING ONION SAUCE

MAKES ABOUT 190 ML (6½ FL OZ)

60 ml (¼ cup) soy sauce

2 tbsp rice (or white) vinegar

6 garlic cloves, crushed

2 tsp caster (superfine) sugar

2 tbsp gochugaru (Korean chilli flakes)

½ tsp freshly ground black pepper

2–3 spring onions (scallions), finely sliced

Combine all the ingredients in a small bowl and stir until the sugar dissolves.

The sauce will keep in an airtight container in the fridge for up to 5 days.

SOY DIPPING SAUCE

MAKES ABOUT 210 ML (7 FL OZ)

1 tbsp fermented soybean sauce

2½ tbsp soy sauce

1½ tbsp sweet soy sauce

80 g (2¾ oz) young ginger, grated

1½ tbsp white vinegar

juice of ½ lime

2 tbsp chopped red and green bird's eye chillies

Combine all the ingredients except the chillies in a small bowl.

Add 1½ tablespoons of water, mix well and check the seasoning; adjust the amount of sweetness and sourness to your liking. Add the chopped chilli to taste just before serving.

The dipping sauce will keep in an airtight container in the fridge for up to 1 week.

HAINANESE KAYA

MAKES ABOUT 500 ML (2 CUPS)

3 eggs

200 g (7 oz) caster (superfine) sugar, plus 60 g (2 oz) extra

250 ml (1 cup) coconut milk

3 pandan leaves, knotted

Crack the eggs into a mixing bowl and whisk in the sugar until combined. Add the coconut milk and stir well, then strain the mixture through a fine-mesh sieve into a stainless steel bowl and add the pandan leaves.

Set the bowl over a saucepan of simmering water over medium heat for 7–10 minutes, stirring occasionally, until the mixture starts to warm and thicken. Reduce the heat to the lowest setting and stir often to prevent any lumps forming. After about 10 minutes the jam should be thick enough to coat the back of a wooden spoon. Remove the bowl from the pan and stir constantly for another minute. Set aside.

Tip the extra sugar into a clean heavy-based saucepan over medium heat and add 1 teaspoon of water. Without stirring, let the sugar dissolve and turn into an amber caramel, then quickly drizzle it into the jam mixture and mix well to combine.

Allow to cool completely, then place the jam in an airtight container. The kaya will keep in the fridge for up to 1 month.

PICKLED CARROT AND DAIKON

MAKES 1.3 KG (2 LB 14 OZ)

1 kg (2 lb 3 oz) carrots, cut into matchsticks

300 g (10½ oz) daikon (white radish), cut into matchsticks

PICKLE LIQUID

150 ml (5 fl oz) white vinegar

100 g (3½ oz) caster (superfine) sugar

To make the pickle liquid, combine the vinegar and sugar in a bowl and add 100 ml (3½ fl oz) of water. Stir until the sugar dissolves.

Rinse the daikon and carrot under warm running water for 5 minutes, then drain thoroughly and pat dry with paper towel. Transfer to a large plastic container or non-reactive bowl.

Pour the pickle liquid over the vegetables and set aside in the fridge for 2 days, after which time the pickles will be ready to use.

The pickled carrot and daikon will keep in the fridge for up to 2 weeks.

BISI BELE BATH MASALA

MAKES ABOUT 50 G (1¾ OZ)

1 tsp urad dal (black gram)

1 tsp chana dal (split chickpeas)

2 tbsp coriander seeds

1 tsp cumin seeds

1 tsp fenugreek seeds

5 cm (2 in) piece cinnamon stick

3–4 cloves

½ tsp black peppercorns

½ mace

2 cardamom pods

1 small marathi moggu (optional; see Note)

1 tsp neutral oil

1 tbsp dried coconut shaves

4 dried Kashmiri red chillies

Heat a frying pan over low heat and add both dals. Stirring often, dry-roast for about 2 minutes until browned, then transfer to a tray to cool.

Dry-roast the coriander, cumin and fenugreek seeds in the same pan until fragrant, about a minute, and transfer to the same tray. Now dry-roast the cinnamon, cloves, peppercorns, mace, cardamom pods and marathi moggu, if using, until aromatic, about a minute, and transfer to the tray.

Heat the oil in the pan and add the coconut and chillies, roasting for about 2 minutes until crisp. Transfer to the tray and allow to cool completely, then use a spice grinder or mortar and pestle to process into fine powder.

Pour the masala into an airtight container. It can be kept until it loses its fragrance.

NOTE: Marathi moggu is best described as a caper and is common in Indian cooking. It can be found in Indian supermarkets and spice shops.

SEASONED ENGLISH SPINACH

SERVES 4

250–300 g (5–6 cups)
English spinach
(about 1 bunch)

1 garlic clove,
finely chopped

1 tsp sesame oil

1 tsp toasted sesame
seeds

Prepare a bowl of iced water. Bring a large saucepan of water to the boil over high heat. Blanch the spinach for 30 seconds, then drain and immediately refresh in the iced water. Leave to chill in the water for 10 minutes, then drain and trim off the roots.

Spread the spinach out on a chopping board, then cut the stems and leaves into 5 cm (2 in) lengths. Gather the spinach with both hands and squeeze firmly to remove any excess water. Loosen up the leaves and transfer to a mixing bowl. Add the garlic, sesame oil and sesame seeds and toss everything together with your hands. Season to taste with salt.

SAUTEED ZUCCHINI

SERVES 4

2 zucchini (courgettes),
cut into 3 mm (⅛ in)
thick slices

⅛ tsp salt, plus extra for
seasoning

1 tbsp neutral oil

2 garlic cloves, finely
chopped

Toss the zucchini and salt in a bowl, then set aside for 1 hour. Strain the zucchini in a fine-mesh sieve.

Heat the oil in a frying pan over medium heat. Add the zucchini and fry gently for 2–3 minutes or until just tender. Add the garlic, 2 tablespoons of water and season to taste with salt. Saute for another minute, or until the zucchini is softened but not mushy. Transfer to a plate and cool until room temperature.

SEASONED SOYBEAN SPROUTS

SERVES 4

1 tsp salt

450 g (1 lb) soybean sprouts

2 garlic cloves, finely chopped

2 tsp toasted sesame seeds

1 spring onion (scallion), thinly sliced

1 tbsp fish sauce, to taste

2 tsp sesame oil

2 tsp gochugaru (Korean chilli flakes; optional)

Prepare a bowl of iced water. Combine 1 litre (1 qt) of water and the salt in a large saucepan and bring to the boil over medium–high heat. Add the bean sprouts and boil, covered, for 5 minutes or until softened and translucent. Do not remove the lid during cooking or the sprouts will have an unpleasant aftertaste – if the water boils over, reduce the heat.

Once cooked, drain the sprouts immediately and refresh in the iced water for 5 minutes. Drain, shaking off any excess water, and transfer to a mixing bowl. Add the garlic, sesame seeds, spring onion, fish sauce, sesame oil and, if desired, gochugaru and mix everything together well.

PORK LOAF

SERVES 4

2 eggs

500 g (1 lb 2 oz) minced (ground) pork

50 g (1¾ oz) wood ear mushrooms, roughly chopped

60 g (2 oz) glass (cellophane) noodles, rehydrated in cold water for 1 hour, drained and cut into short lengths

1 Asian shallot, finely chopped

3 tbsp fish sauce

1 tbsp caster (superfine) sugar

pinch of ground white pepper

Separate the eggs and set aside the yolks. Beat the egg whites in a large bowl until airy, then add the remaining ingredients, except the yolks, and mix well.

Place a large bamboo steamer over a saucepan of boiling water. Line a 25 cm × 12 cm (10 in × 4¾ in) loaf (bar) tin with foil and spoon in the pork loaf mixture. Transfer the tin to the steamer and steam, covered, for 30 minutes. Open the lid and brush the reserved egg yolks on top of the loaf, then steam with the lid off for a further 5 minutes. Remove from the heat and enjoy.

INDEX

Published in 2024 by Smith Street Books
Naarm (Melbourne) | Australia
smithstreetbooks.com

ISBN: 978-1-9230-4908-6

Smith Street Books respectfully acknowledges the Wurundjeri
People of the Kulin Nation, who are the Traditional Owners of the
land on which we work, and we pay our respects to their Elders
past and present.

Publisher: Paul McNally
Editor and text: Avery Hayes
Design concept: George Saad
Design layout: Megan Ellis
Photographer: Emily Weaving
Stylist: Bridget Wald
Food preparation: Caroline Griffiths & Allison Kekovski
Proofreader: Pam Dunne
Indexer: Helena Holmgren

Printed & bound in China by C&C Offset Printing Co., Ltd.

Book 313
10 9 8 7 6 5 4 3 2 1